FINANCING YOUR FREEDOM

THE BLUEPRINT FOR PERSONAL FINANCE

This publication is designed to provide general information regarding the subjects covered. It may be used for reference but does not replace in-depth financial planning to fit your unique scenario. We share concepts we have used along with others that have had favorable outcomes but does not guarantee future performance of your investments or businesses.

The author has taken reasonable precautions in the preparation of this book and believes the information presented is accurate as of the date it was written. However, neither the author nor publisher assumes responsibility for any errors or omissions. Please use due diligence and caution when making life choices, investing and starting businesses, especially with funds from investors.

We recommend hiring a team of competent advisors and mentors to give guidance along the way. Familiarize yourself with tax laws, accounting principles, and SEC guidelines when raising capital, offering securities, and starting or purchasing businesses.

Remain open-minded and studious, realize the mistakes along the way, while minimizing losses and gaining valuable information in the process. There will be challenges to overcome and downtimes on the roller coaster to your goals but that is what makes for an interesting ride.

Revision A Published February 28, 2021
Paperback ISBN: 978-1-7356312-0-2
E-book ISBN: 978-1-7356312-1-9
Copyright 2020 "Financing Your Freedom"

CONTENTS

CONTENTS

PREFACE
CURRENT STATE OF AFFAIRS

It's important to know the rules of a game if you are ever to level up and beat it. The game is generating sustainable income and the outcome is called retirement or financial freedom to many people. It is when investment income funds your lifestyle and allows the freedom to do what you deem important.

Unfortunately, financial education is minimal in our public education system and most courses are not designed to help you retire. My goal is to keep this book simple and provide productive concepts that will empower you to make better financial decisions. I will provide an overview of many important ideas and leave recommendations at the end of the book if you want to learn more about specific subjects. Let's get into it...

There are millions of Americans living paycheck to paycheck and 69% have $1000 or less in savings (**www.fool.com/retirement**). These statistics are mind-blowing and the catalyst that drove me to write this book.

There is also a pension crisis that faces America and the elderly population. According to USA Today, the typical state pension only has enough money to pay 70% of what it owes. This is an average and many state funds are in much worse shape.

Americans aged 35 to 54 average $133,000 of debt per household. These numbers look challenging collectively but can be even worse on an individual basis. Thestreet.com states that Americans aged 60 to 69 have a median balance of $62,000 in their 401k accounts, which isn't going to last very long.

A vast majority are relying on Social Security to take them through retirement and that system is massively underfunded, just as the pensions are. The Social Security Administration has already released information stating that as early as 2035, they will have to reduce payouts by 20% if no adjustments are made.

The US government debt has exceeded $25 trillion and broke a record for the largest historical deficit in 2020. The World Bank stated that we are in the deepest global recession in decades. This reckless policy of currency printing and deficit spending will continue to be a burden on its citizens until we decide on a sound fiscal and monetary policy.

Do you see the sense of urgency and the importance of taking financial measures to protect yourself and your family? If you do not choose responsibility and independence, you may move forward into a Universal Basic Income for people who couldn't take care of themselves. This is a form of welfare given to you each month and will be very challenging to gain independence from.

We have to face the facts if we want to create something better for ourselves and the next generation.

Don't just believe me, I challenge you to do your research on the current state of affairs and economic trends. If we wake up and start looking at important things, we will realize what is holding us back and how we can move forward productively...

PART I:
BASICS OF FINANCE

CHAPTER 1
RICH, WEALTHY, POOR, & BROKE

There is a common misconception that rich and wealthy can be used synonymously. I focus on vocabulary because words are powerful and pave the way for our actions. At the end of this book, I have created a glossary that defines some of the common words that are necessary for financial literacy.

If you use the wrong words and make poor decisions, it can lead to a slippery slope of poverty and financial destruction. Although, by paying attention to what you spend your time and resources on, you can change your financial status in a relatively short time. Daily wise and consistent decisions can transform your life into something you never thought was possible. It is your story and you are in control of the narrative.

Someone in my line of work opened my eyes by stating that I was one injury away from being completely broke with no means to take care of myself and my family. Understanding you are a vulnerable human makes you appreciate creating income from investments and not solely reliant upon your labor. This reminder also keeps me honest and productive with the time I do have. It is important to know what wealth is and how to manage systems that pay you income instead of only trading time for currency.

Every individual has a different appetite for finance, along with a perspective that can be vastly different. I will attempt to simplify these terms so we can set a standard and hone our perspective.

The main difference between being rich and wealthy is time and sustainability.

If we measure wealth by the time that we have to live life on the terms of our choice, I believe most will see they are fairly broke. How long can you survive at your current spending levels from the investment income you have coming in?

A rich person may have a lot of cash and many vehicles, houses, and toys while a wealthy person will have multiple income streams that pay for their desired lifestyle. We can view wealth as the management of systems that sustainably generates income to fund our lifestyle; whereas riches can be amassed or inherited and depleted in a relatively short amount of time.

I like to use the comparison of a couple of famous basketball players to see the difference between riches and wealth. Allen Iverson was a famous basketball player that amassed $200M throughout his career and eventually ended up filing for bankruptcy because he couldn't pay his debts, one of which was a $900,000 debt to a jeweler, according to TMZ. Fortunately, later Iverson has made some deals to get out of his financial slump but this is a good example of being rich, going broke, and then rebounding.

Let's look at Shaquille O' Neal who earned a similar salary but now has multiplied the income through investing, which we call wealth. Shaq started on a spending spree like most professional athletes but has corrected course and now owns 17 Auntie Anne's pretzel franchises, a Krispy Kreme franchise, several restaurants, gyms, and car washes. One has spent his riches while the other has created wealth and still receives $60M per year after retirement. He has created systems and employed people that will outlive him while yielding a surplus of income for the rest of his life. O' Neal has stated that one key to his sustainability is by living off of only 25% of his income, which we will dive into later.

The key is to know how much income you need each month to finance your freedom. Look at your expenses and get very clear on how much you spend and what assets can produce that amount.

It seems many people want to make a lot of money and to purchase items that make them appear rich, instead of working on strategies that generate income for the duration of their lives.

If you know that you just want to acquire a large sum of cash to purchase liabilities to have fun, that is fine as long as you know the consequences that come along with that. It is not sustainable and is not fulfilling in the long term. Look at interviews from people who have amassed riches but did not do things that were fulfilling to their soul and what they believed in.

You will find a fair percentage of these individuals who are miserable, lonely, or not fully satisfied with their lives. This may be difficult to understand but others who have experienced this know what I'm referring to. The book "The Second Mountain" by David Brooks, along with several others, inspired me and challenged my ideas of being rich without a purpose. It made me realize that life is more fulfilling when helping others within our lives. It also made me understand that when we create and add value we contribute to the betterment of the community.

If you focus solely on making money and not the value that it can bring to your life and others, your life will probably feel that something is missing.

The main difference between poor and broke is mindset.

As we discussed earlier, a good example of going broke is a lot of professional athletes. Sports Illustrated did a study that showed 75% of NFL players go broke within two years of leaving professional sports and 60% of NBA players are broke within five years. This is astonishing because these people earn millions of dollars, year after year, and still never figure out how to manage it. At the end of the day, it doesn't matter how much you make if you are spending it faster.

Being or going broke simply means that you had something of value but have lost it due to an event or series of events. While this is unfortunate, it can be fixed through proper planning, diligent effort, and investing. Broke is a temporary problem for someone who has the right mindset and can generate income by providing value to the community.

In a similar term, we use the word poor to describe someone who has never had anything of financial value and generally refers to a mindset flaw. I realize that we are products of our environments and our limiting beliefs but with today's technology, we can overcome adversity faster and with less effort than ever. Poor is a mindset that allows you to be a victim of outside circumstances and not taking responsibility for your life. If you take ownership of your life and realize you are the reason you are currently in the situation, it leaves you to deal with the problem and correct it or continue getting the same results.

You will hear it time and again "Oh look what happened to me today" or "With my luck, I'm sure it won't work". These are ideas that form beliefs and the program that runs our lives. Your reality is a reflection of your belief system and we must break these habits of belief if we are ever to get out of the current situation.

I do not look down on anyone and realize bad things happen to good people but I'm a firm believer that we must work diligently to rise out of a bad situation if we desire better outcomes. If you want to be poor, more power to you but I just want everyone to know it is a choice and there are alternatives.

Some people do not see value in amassing fortunes but we all require financial resources to provide necessities and fund our life's work. I challenge you to understand this concept and figure out how much you need to generate monthly to fund your desired lifestyle. Everyone's numbers will be a little different so you must be true to yourself and document your expenses while being resourceful with income.

Over the next several chapters, we will discuss the basics. These topics include the history of our money, bank accounts, credit accounts, different types of income, expenses, assets, liabilities, and taxes.

In Chapter 7, I will show you how to take account of your current situation with the income statement and balance sheet. Feel free to skip ahead if you are a more advanced reader and are ready to run your numbers, expand your knowledge on investments, and make progress on the path to Financing your Freedom!

CHAPTER 2
MONEY & BANKING

History of our Money

The first official money dates back to around 680 B.C and was created out of a mixture of gold and silver, called Electrum in Lydia, which is now a part of Turkey. We can find gold used before this going back to the ancient Egyptians several thousand years B.C, but Lydia is recorded as the first official standardized form of money.

Before the discovery of precious metals as money, barter was used primarily as a means of exchange between people. Barter still works fine for some accounts, but the creation of a standard was a huge improvement to our society. There are a few characteristics that money is supposed to have and they are durability, portability, divisibility, uniformity, acceptability, and a store of value.

For example, a 1-ounce gold coin through history was durable, easy to carry, could be divided into smaller denominations with other gold or silver coins, was uniform in shape and size, readily accepted as money, along with being a stable store of value over time. This is a prime example of what money is supposed to be and what it has been for a long part of history. The dollar or other fiat currencies we use today have many of these money characteristics, except for the store of value.

Beginning in 1795 in the US, gold and silver coins were being used as a medium of exchange for transactions. The first 3 denominations of gold coins in America were the $10 Eagle, $5 Half Eagle, and $2.50 Quarter Eagle, along with silver denominations of one dollar, half dollar, quarter dollar, dime, and half dime. They had no dollar value on them at the time because gold and silver were money and measured only by the weight and purity of the coin. The original silver to gold ratio was 15 ounces of silver being equal to 1 ounce of gold.

Until the Civil War broke out, gold and silver were the normal transactional form of money and there was no legal tender paper money in the US. The main reason it changed during the Civil War was the need to debase the money and spend more than it received in tax payments on the war efforts. You can see this common trend throughout history.

1862 brought about a new system that would allow the United States Note to be used as legal tender instead of physical gold and silver coin. Legal tender is the primary means of exchange within a country and this law would change physical coins to banknotes for public and private debt. This was signed into law by Abraham Lincoln through the First Legal Tender Act. These notes that were overseen by the US Treasury were the first national notes of its kind and set a precedent for future belief in the paper currency we use today.

There were several different kinds of currency during the mid to late 1800s and consisted of notes from many state and national banks, but gold would continue to be the haven form of money that people trusted and held while circulating the paper forms.

The US would go back to fully convertible money into gold on March 14, 1900, through the Gold Standard Act and used silver coins for change. This fixed each dollar to an amount that was equal to 1.5 grams of pure gold and a rate of $20.67 per troy ounce. This was a step back in the right direction but it would not last long...

Franklin Roosevelt signed Executive Order 6102 on April 5th, 1933 which stated if you were a private citizen, you had to turn in all gold over $100 in value to the Federal Reserve and redeem it for $20.67 of Federal Reserve Notes per troy ounce or face possible imprisonment of 10 years or up to $10,000 in fines.

With the passing of the Gold Reserve Act of 1934, it removed the convertibility from paper dollars to gold within the US, along with requiring all gold that was collected by the Federal Reserve to be transferred to the US Treasury. The Treasury then revalued the dollar price of gold to $35 per ounce from $20.67 which increased the value of their holdings immediately by $2.81 billion.

The Bretton Woods agreement of 1944 created a standard that established the US dollar as the global reserve currency. After the agreement, central banks were the only ones that could exchange their currency for gold at a rate of $35 per ounce. This became a problem over the years as countries would call in their gold holdings and start diminishing the gold in storage. Over time, this led to a run for gold and ultimately passing legislation that would remove the convertibility of currency to gold for all nations...

Move to August 15th, 1971 and this was the final straw to getting away from the concept of precious metals as money. Richard Nixon passed legislation where the US would no longer convert currency into gold and therefore changed our money into the fiat currency that we use today, along with every other currency in circulation.

It wasn't until 1974 that it became legal again for private citizens in America to own gold bullion. Since then, we have seen a steady increase in dollar prices of gold. It went from $50 then to nearly $2000 per ounce. It is clear to me that there are still high requests for the confidence of gold and an ever-increasing demand by investors throughout the globe. This same thing is happening with Bitcoin and other alternatives as the demand for fiat currencies is declining.

Today's "Money"

We have been frauded with this "money" we utilize today and a fiat system that has historically failed all empires. I put money in quotes because as we said earlier it is a fiat currency that has the illusion of value. Money is supposed to be a store of value, yet our national currencies are losing value each year.

The US Dollar has currently lost over 95% of its' purchasing power since 1913. This can be shown by the dollar price of gold and the prices of other necessities in life with the Consumer Price Index (CPI). Since 2000, the Euro has devalued 85% when compared to gold. The following webpage explains it in more detail:

https://www.thebalance.com/what-is-the-value-of-a-dollar-today-3306105

One way that we track the strength of the dollar compared to the big six international currencies is through the U.S. Dollar Index (USDX). This index was established in 1973 at a baseline of 100 and tracks the dollar's purchasing power over time compared to the Euro, Swiss Franc, Japanese Yen, Canadian Dollar, British Pound, and Swedish Krona.

This is necessary because currencies are no longer fixed to each other and the value fluctuates over time. If the number drops below 100, the dollar has gotten weaker against the currencies and if it rises above 100, the dollar's purchasing power is increased. Investopedia explains this more at: **https://www.investopedia.com/terms/u/usdx.asp**

If you are saving currency, regardless of the denomination, you are losing purchasing power, year after year. Zimbabwe, the Weimar Republic, and Venezuela are great examples to research if you are not familiar with the effects of hyperinflation.

The more we print currency without solid backing, the more we are stealing from our future. Each new dollar that goes into circulation reduces the purchasing power of the one prior by creating more supply.

There is only about 10% of physical dollars in the US when compared to the total currency supply. The worldwide average is around 8% of physical cash for the total supply of currency. This number will decrease rapidly as fewer commercial banks are required to hold physical cash in their vaults.

Do yourself a favor and take a look at the paper bills or coins you have in your pocket. That is if you are lucky enough to have any cash, considering most people spend only in digital currency with their credit cards or digital wallets. Today's coins are made from a cupronickel alloy that has very little intrinsic value, along with the notes being printed on a mixture of cotton and linen. If people were to stop believing it is valuable and start using alternatives, it could fall to zero because it has minimal intrinsic value.

Up to 1964 in the US, our coins were comprised of 90% silver and gold coins minted up to 1933 were 90% gold. Compare a quarter from 1964 or earlier to the junk they mint now. It looks very similar in design but is a counterfeit version of the sound and responsible money of years past.

A good example to show you how we are being ripped off is to look up the silver melt value of a 1964 quarter compared to the metal melt value of a quarter of today. The 90% silver content of

.072 troy ounces in a 1964 quarter is worth $2.82, whereas a copper and nickel quarter of today has about $.09 of metal value. Which one would you rather have?

We have been getting away from the physical transactions of cash purchases more each year and soon everything could be strictly digital transactions...

Take a look at China now and how they use apps such as WeChat or Alipay to make restaurant reservations, order food, and pay for the food, all with a few touches on the smartphone. There is virtually no cash and a lot of places do not accept credit cards anymore. I believe this could be the next step for the world and then merging this technology with humans through the integration of Artificial Intelligence (AI).

I value the options to pay in cash, cryptocurrency, precious metals, or barter as it gives us choices in case of emergencies or a digital shutdown. Think of it as planning for a hurricane or other disasters that can make life challenging. Having alternatives is a great policy for risk mitigation in most areas of our life.

It will be interesting to see the change in mediums of exchange and what we consider money within the next 20 years. In the meantime, let's take a look at how banking can help us store reserves and some of the things to be cautious of with accounts.

Bank Accounts & Fees

There are a few different types of bank accounts that can be beneficial if you know what to look for in an account. They can also charge ridiculous fees that will lead you to frustration if you aren't careful. When most think of bank accounts they often think of the traditional brick and mortar banks in your local community such as Bank of America or Wells Fargo, where you can visit and conduct business.

While these can still work fine, especially if you prefer face-to-face transactions, online banks are increasing in popularity. They tend to offer a higher savings yield and fewer fees because of the lower operating cost in the online-only experience. Of course, the downside is only being able to interact virtually through the internet. The choice is yours to see what works best for your situation. I recommend using **bankrate.com** or **nerdwallet.com** to search for banks and the fees associated with different accounts.

The most common accounts that people have at any bank are a checking account and a savings account. A **checking account** is an account that is used for everyday transactions. To open either of these accounts, you should be 18 years of age with a photo ID and a social security number. These are the most common requirements if you are opening an account by yourself.

You can have an Automated Teller Machine (ATM) card linked to the checking account where you can spend the cash electronically in person, online, or you can write checks to pay as well. You can also use ATM cards to withdraw or deposit cash at participating ATM locations. Be sure to ask about **ATM fees** if you use a machine outside of the host bank network.

Most banks usually offer some electronic sending methods such as Zelle, where you can transfer amounts up to $2,500 per week for free or wire transfer any amount for a fee of around $30. There are also third-party apps such as Cash App, PayPal, or Venmo that you can download on your phone to transfer if your bank does not offer this service.

There are many different types of fees associated with banking and it is important to learn them if you want to keep more of your hard-earned money. Annually, banks take in over $11 billion just in overdraft fees. **Overdraft fees** or non-sufficient funds fees are when your account has less money than the transaction cost. If this happens, the bank usually charges a fee to cover you until the item clears or charges a fee and does not honor the transaction. Either way, the important thing to remember is to track your expenses and do not get in the negative because they will charge you even more money in fees.

At most banks, you can link a credit card or savings account to your checking account to avoid these overdraft fees and they will honor the transaction if you make the mistake of going negative on a transaction. This is called overdraft protection and I have my credit card linked to my checking account, just in case I make the mistake of spending more than my checking account balance; this allows the payment to go through and then I pay the credit card off that month.

If you travel often you want to be cautious of **foreign transaction fees**. This occurs if your checking account is a US account denominated in dollars and you go to spend in Euros or any other foreign currency. Some banks will charge up to 3% of the transaction cost in foreign transaction fees and/or a flat-rate amount for the conversion. This can be an insane amount if you are using this continuously on a trip, so be sure to get an account that does not charge foreign transaction fees. Pay in the host currency wherever you are to avoid these conversion rates and transaction fees.

Capital One was one of the first companies I saw that offered these no-fee cards but you can shop around on **wallethub.com** or **nerdwallet.com** and compare the best credit cards with no foreign transaction fees, best cashback or reward points, along with seeing what fees may be charged.

Some banks also charge a **monthly service fee or a minimum balance fee.** Be sure to look for these when shopping around on the above resources and finding a product that works well for you. You shouldn't have to pay a bank usurious fees to store your money so be smart when you are shopping around. Doing some research on the internet will be an efficient way to compare banks and credit cards that fit your needs while minimizing fees.

Today's **savings accounts** are not what they were in times past when the banks would pay a fair amount of interest if you kept your cash with them. A savings account was designed as an account to store the excess of what you didn't need for everyday transactions in your checking account. It also helps to keep these funds separate when creating reserves so you aren't tempted to spend them. There may be a minimum balance on these accounts along with a limited number of withdrawals or transfers per month.

Annual Percentage Yield (APY) is the annual rate at which you earn interest on the savings account. Today, the average savings yield for brick-and-mortar banks is around .05%, while the lower overhead, online-only banks may pay out .5% annually. Regardless, neither option is going to let you sit back and drink your favorite beverage while accruing high interest of years past.

If you want to try to earn a little more on interest you can ask your local or online banks about **Money Market accounts** or **Certificate of Deposit** accounts. Make sure you get all the details on fees and how long you have to let the funds sit in there because you may not have access to these dollars for a while. These accounts tend to tie up funds for minimum length requirements or a minimum daily balance requirement.

For business needs, I prefer a local brick-and-mortar bank. I use a few personal and business checking/savings accounts for face-to-face transactions. These help me make easy work out of paying vendors, salaries, utilizing lines of credit, and other banking needs.

I have established a rapport and it seems to be an efficient method for me.

I also have a personal checking with Charles Schwab that saves me on foreign transaction/ATM fees, as well as an online-only savings account with Ally Bank. I use their online banking for ease of use on weekly savings transfers and bill pay to stay organized with payments. Having multiple accounts and banks ensures the business is kept separate from personal accounts, as well as having backup accounts when traveling.

What is Inflation?

Inflation is the rate at which the price of a basket of goods and services in an economy increases over time. This is reported annually by the U.S. Bureau of Labor Statistics through a metric called the Consumer Price Index (CPI).

The Federal Reserve central bank attempts to maintain a 2% target inflation rate by adjusting interest rates over time. By reducing rates, people are more likely to spend, which increases inflation. By increasing rates, there is an opposite effect.

Today, all central banks create fiat currency that we use in everyday exchange. A fiat currency is a national currency that is not backed by gold or other valuables. As central banks increase this fiat currency supply, the previous dollars become less valuable by increasing the total supply.

It has often been referred to as a silent tax that erodes our purchasing power over time. The good news is that we are going to learn about investments in Chapter 9 to help reduce this.

CHAPTER 3
CREDIT & DEBT

What is Principal & Interest?

Principal is the amount borrowed. **Interest** is the additional amount that is paid to a lender for borrowing.

As you make payments, some will go to interest and the rest will reduce the principal. Interest can be a fixed or variable rate and is expressed as a percentage. APR is the "annual percentage rate" of interest that we pay. In a fixed-rate loan, the interest rate doesn't change as opposed to a variable or adjustable-rate that fluctuates over time.

The higher the interest rate, the more you will pay in interest over the life of the principal. As time goes on and you increase your financial responsibility, your credit score should increase and allow you to grasp lower interest rates.

Many loans use a system called amortization which means the payment is the same each month, consisting of principal and interest, and extinguishes the debt with the last payment. One interesting thing about amortization is that while the payment is the same each month, you pay more interest in the beginning years because interest is calculated on the principal balance. As you reduce the principal, the interest portion of the payment will be reduced.

I recommend experimenting with an amortization calculator to adjust the principal, interest rates, and the length of the loan to understand the process more. You can save a fortune on interest and years on your home loan, auto loans, student loans, and more if you learn how interest is accumulated and make principal payments early on the loan. Check out **www.amortization-calc.com** for a calculator that will help you understand how much you can save on interest by making additional principal payments on any installment loans.

Credit cards are a good example of compounding interest and a way many people get trapped in debt over time. Compound interest accrues interest on the principal and the accrued interest over time, whereas simple interest accrues on the principal only.

Compound interest can get very confusing, so I will just recommend researching and comparing simple and compounding interest calculators to see how they differ. The key to credit cards is to pay them off within the 30-day window of use, so you accrue no interest at all. They can be valuable tools if you use them this way and do not pay any interest on your purchases.

These are the basics of how loans and credit accounts work. It is important to know how to calculate the interest you will pay or receive over time so you can choose wisely. Without the basic understanding, you may pay higher than market interest rates or not receive market rates when lending to others.

What is the difference between Credit and Debt?

Credit is the ability to borrow, while **debt** is the result of borrowing. For example, if your credit is deemed to be good, banks and other financial institutions will extend credit in the form of credit cards, auto loans, student loans, housing loans, personal loans, etc. When you utilize credit for a car or a home, that is now called debt. Debt is something, typically money, that is owed or due to someone else. It is an obligation to repay an institution in the future, in exchange for what you receive today.

Regardless, if you are an individual or a business, the basic principles of credit and debt work the same. Personal credit scores range from 300 to 850 and are tracked by Experian, Equifax, and Transunion. The score is a representation of your responsibility with credit and is based on several factors. A few things that affect your score are the number and types of accounts on your report, payment activity over time, balances on your credit accounts, accounts in delinquency, credit inquiries, and the length of time you have had credit accounts available.

Business credit is usually tracked by Dun & Bradstreet, Experian, and Equifax and gives an overall credit picture of your business. The credit range for a business is usually 0 to 100. The concept is the same in that the above factors impact the score and creditworthiness as a borrower.

It is recommended to keep your total consumer debt below 30% of your gross income (before tax). This includes all debt from home loans, auto loans, student loans, and other credit accounts. Lenders look at this metric as the Debt to Income Ratio (DTI). It is a ratio calculated by dividing your total monthly debt payments by your monthly gross income and is a quick snapshot of how you manage your finances. If your monthly debt payments are $2000 and your monthly income before taxes is $5000, your DTI is .4 or 40% of your gross income going to debt payments.

Keeping debt below 30% of your income is a recommendation by most lenders. The lower your debt to income, the more income you have available to multiply through investments.

Six Factors that Affect Credit & How to Increase your Score

It is important to open credit accounts early in life so that you can increase the **age of credit history**. This is the average time that your credit accounts have been open and each new account added will reduce the average age of the accounts. This is a big factor when lenders look at your credit so be sure to leave credit accounts open, even if you are frustrated with them or do not plan to use them often. When I first started, I closed a few credit cards that could have increased my credit age and overall score.

Once you establish accounts, it is imperative to **pay the accounts on time** each month to build a rapport and to allow for future credit expansion. This is one of the most important factors over time that can help your credit. I like to put all of my accounts in a tracking spreadsheet and pay bills bi-weekly so I stay on top of payment due dates. You could also input the due dates into the calendar on your phone as a reminder. I also use online bill pay to easily pay creditors each month. If you can't manage a $300 credit account on time, why would anyone loan you more?

The **total number of accounts** plays a factor in your overall score as well. The higher the number of accounts that show payment history on time will increase your score and creditworthiness. The more diverse accounts that you have will show you know how to manage credit across a range of products. The key is paying all accounts on time and showing responsibility.

Delinquencies and Collection Accounts are the worst thing for your credit. If you are ever in situations where you can't make payments, it is very important to make arrangements with the creditors to ensure the account does not go into delinquency or collections. This looks very bad to creditors and is a common way people get into financial trouble. If you do go into collections, create a plan to make payments to extinguish this as soon as possible.

Even if you pay collections accounts in full, they can remain on your report for up to 7 years, so stay on time and do some research on how you can get these cleared after you have paid them in full. Some nonpayment of loans may allow the creditor to come after other items you own, so make sure you read the fine print and understand the terms of the loan before you sign.

High Balances on your credit account over 30% of the account limit play a large factor in your credit score as well. It is important to manage the balances and don't become overleveraged with debt that you cannot repay in a fair amount of time. You may see this referred to as credit card utilization rate. Too much debt on your credit accounts shows potential danger for future lenders and that you can't manage your credit responsibly.

Credit inquiries affect your credit score and are seen as a potential risk to lenders. An inquiry is when a creditor pulls your credit report to see if you are worthy of a new account. These inquiries usually stay on your credit report for up to 2 years and creditors view many inquiries as someone potentially being risky or in financial troubles, so be careful with how many accounts you apply for. When I started, I applied for several credit cards at one time so the inquiries were close together and also showed them dropping off the credit report about the same time in two years.

How to Analyze your Credit

I use a site called **www.creditkarma.com** to track my credit monthly and to ensure no one steals my electronic identity. Many sites can help you track your credit that are free, such as credit karma and **creditsesame.com**, or paid sites such as **www.privacyguard.com**. You may have free access through some credit cards or bank accounts such as Capital One or Chase, where they offer free monitoring services. These resources will update and track your score weekly and you are authorized one free complete credit report each year by visiting **www.annualcreditreport.com**.

The above-mentioned items comprise your score and it increasing or decreasing over time. It takes time to build credit so be sure to have patience, especially if you are rebuilding bad credit or do not currently have established credit. You will realize the value of good credit as you increase your financial intelligence and get better rates in the future. It is an investment in the future of yourself.

Types of Consumer Credit

There are many types of credit and they are also referred to as loans, lines of credit, or credit accounts. Regardless of the type of account requested, your credit rating will determine the interest rate and amount of credit extended to you. It is important to understand how credit works from the paragraphs above and see what you need to do to increase your rating over time and maintain a great score.

Look at your life and think about how credit can help you. Opening useful credit accounts early play a vital role in establishing credit, which is a major issue because a lot of people simply do not have any credit. More than half of America is credit invisible or has poor credit.

It is recommended to become familiar with the different types of consumer/business loans and the language they use in lending if you plan to utilize their services. Look at the differences between fixed interest rates vs. variable or adjustable rates and different repayment periods.

Consumer debt in America currently stands around $14 trillion, comprising of home loans, student loans, auto loans, and credit card debt. These are in order of highest to lowest debt levels and we will discuss each one below.

Home Loans

Home loans makeup 68% of all US consumer debt and are the largest account of consumer credit. A home loan uses the property as collateral for the currency you receive to purchase it. The lender can foreclose on the home and require you to move out if you do not make payments toward the loan.

There are several types of consumer **home loans**, with the most popular being the VA (Veterans Affairs), FHA (Federal Housing Administration), USDA (US Department of Agriculture), and conventional loans. The first 3 are government-insured loans and the last is a conventional loan where the lender takes liability for the loan. Once the conventional loan is completed, it is usually sold to Fannie Mae, Freddie Mac, or another financial institution so the commercial bank can lend more money. VA loans are only available for those who are qualified members of the Armed Forced or have separated, while the other loans may be available to anyone.

Currently, VA has a 0% down payment, FHA and USDA have a 3.5% down payment, and most conventional loans require between 3 to 5% down, depending on your creditworthiness. These numbers are based if it will be your primary residence and does not apply to investment properties. Current interest rates are around 3% for excellent credit and go up from there. These rates fluctuate over time with the Prime Rate. You can use most of these loans for any residential property ranging from a single-family home to a multi-unit residential property up to 4 units, where you will live in one of the units and can lease out the additional units, if you choose.

You will often time be offered a fixed-rate loan which indicates the interest rate on the loan will be fixed for the duration of the repayment period. The repayment period is typically a 15-year fixed or a 30-year fixed loan. This is the easiest type of loan to deal with and the monthly payments will always be the same until you extinguish the debt in full. I highly recommend fixed-rate, low-interest loans, especially for non-experienced buyers.

The other option for home loans is adjustable-rate mortgages, also known as ARM. These loans usually have a fixed introductory period from 3, 5, 7, or 10 years with an adjustment period after the initial fixed term. A 5/1 ARM simply means that the first 5 years are going to be a fixed interest rate and the 1 indicates the interest rate can adjust 1 time per year after that. These loans are commonly amortized over a 30-year term as well. You should be careful with these because even a small increase in rates can have an increase in your monthly payment.

A lot of the loans created for borrowers before 2008 were adjustable-rate mortgages and when interest rates increased many people could no longer make the payments or refinance because of dropping real estate values and negative equity. Unless you have proper reserves to cover at least 6 months and a good understanding, it is probably wise to stay away from these adjustable-rate loans.

I encourage you to look at a mortgage calculator such as the one at **www.amortization-calc.com** to understand the payment. You will be able to see how much of your payment is going to principal and how much is going to interest, along with strategizing on how to save.

Look at the cost of owning a home versus the cost of renting a home. You can do this by inputting the home price, interest rate, length of loan, taxes, and insurance costs into a mortgage calculator to arrive at the total monthly payment. Tax amounts are public records and can be looked up through the county website where the property resides. You can call an insurance agent to get a quote on the cost of insurance per year.

Take the Principal, Interest, Taxes, & Insurance (PITI) into account, and also don't forget to create a monthly allowance for repairs, utilities, and general upkeep of the home. Calculate these numbers and arrive at a total monthly cost for homeownership. Look online at **Zillow.com** or call a local property manager and ask what average rents are in that area. Ask if any utilities or garbage pickup is included and you will have an idea which method is a better value.

The next question you need to answer is "Do I want the responsibility of homeownership?" Renting is sometimes a better option for people. If you are in a career where you travel often, it may be better to rent the places where you are, instead of renting out your home or making the payment when you are gone. Renting also comes with less responsibility as the maintenance costs are paid for by the landlord. Most people don't consider the costs of homeownership other than the monthly payment of principal and interest. You also have maintenance, garbage pickup, landscaping, utilities, and property taxes, as we mentioned above.

This is oftentimes one of the most important decisions people make in life and it warrants a fair amount of calculation before you jump into a decision. I have done both for various chapters of my life and what made more sense at the time. I like the idea of renting where I live currently because I tend to move often and travel a lot, but I own the properties that I lease as investments. In the future when I reduce my travel, I will probably purchase another primary residence. The choice is yours but it's smart to look at both ways and what makes more sense to you and your family at the time.

Student Loans

US households with student loan debt average $47,671 and accounts for 11% of all consumer debt. These loans help individuals finance the costs associated with higher education. There are 3 different types of loans consisting of federal, private, and refinance. 92% of all student loans are federal loans that cannot be extinguished through bankruptcy. It is very important to understand the terms of the loan before you put your name on the agreement.

I urge you to take a look at the cost of student loans compared to the income you will receive annually in the career that correlates with education. It should be a risk–reward calculation to determine if it is worth pursuing. Government-backed education loans can be easy to get but that does not mean they are easy to get rid of, especially if you are working in a career that doesn't pay well.

One idea to minimize student loans is to apply for grants or scholarships that will help offset the high cost of college. There are also ways to start in a community college or lower-cost alternatives to get the basic courses out of the way while building your GPA and educational credentials that may help you qualify for a grant or scholarship in the future.

Perform your due diligence while searching for a major and what you want to do with your life. It seems most people have forgotten about trade schools and the productive sectors of the economy such as pilots, auto mechanics, carpenters, plumbers, and HVAC technicians. You also do not have to attend college to be successful in today's world. You could work as an intern to learn the skills, while possibly earning a wage.

There are so many services that you can provide with certificates or hands-on training, such as an e-commerce business, web page designer, real estate sales, hairstylist, auto mechanic, social media marketer, or vehicle detailing. If you do not have many skills, look around and see how you can get the necessary skills without going into large amounts of debt.

The military is also a viable option, even if just for the short term, where you can gain skills and get your education paid for. I gained valuable career and leadership skills in the Air Force and they helped build a solid foundation that got me where I am today.

There are many options if we just stop to think through them and do not rush into a situation. If you already have high amounts of student loans it is important to come up with a solution where you can create a payment arrangement that works for you. As we stated in the credit section, nonpayment can stay on your credit report for up to 7 years. If you are in a position where you have high loans and low wages, the best option may be to defer the payments until you can increase your means. Creativity is the best remedy for a bad situation and you must take the problem head-on to come up with a solution.

Auto Loans

An auto loan is a loan that uses an automobile as collateral. If you do not pay these loans, the lender can repossess the vehicle and choose to resale it to recover the losses. A big-name car dealer such as Toyota or Ford can finance the vehicle directly through their in-house finance department or you may use a traditional lender such as Bank of America or your local credit union. There are also "buy here pay here" car lots that generally charge very high interest, so be cautious of these types of places.

44% of all Americans rely on auto loans to finance their vehicles and these loans comprise 10% of all US consumer debt. We are currently seeing six to seven-year auto loans with low interest that help reduce the monthly payments so consumers can afford the payments.

More auto loans than ever are upside down with negative equity because of the longer repayment periods. Most people are simply not paying enough down on the loans compared to the time where the vehicle needs major servicing or replacement. A lot of people are trading in vehicles where they have negative equity because they did not put much of a down payment and then roll the negative equity into their new loans. This is becoming a huge problem where people keep kicking the can down the road.

I recommend looking at the Kelley Blue Book Value and NADA guides that can give you an idea of the market value of your current vehicle or a vehicle you are shopping for. If you know what the value should be, you will be more cognizant of the prices they are showing you and the offer you may get for your current vehicle. You can also look at the cost of owning a car versus leasing a car.

The average first-year depreciation loss on new cars is 20%, so I choose to never purchase a brand-new car. I will let someone take at least a 20% loss on the vehicle and I will purchase a vehicle within five years old. It depends on how knowledgeable you are in mechanics or if you know a reputable mechanic, but it is generally cheaper to repair a vehicle that is a few years old when compared to buying a new car that depreciates rapidly within the first few years.

It's also important to look at the loan terms they are offering and what the interest rate and length of loan are. Dealers will often sell you on the idea that you can make the payment, but it is prudent to look at the total cost of the loan and how long you will be handcuffed to that payment. Salesmen care about making commissions because that is what pays their bills. I propose finding a reasonably priced, pre-owned, reliable vehicle that you can put at least 10% down on and finance with low-interest loans or pay cash for it. It's a depreciating liability and should never be considered an asset unless you use the vehicle to create income.

Credit Cards

45% of all Americans carry a balance on their credit cards each year. This is perpetuated by the entitlement mentality and that we all deserve things right now and can pay for them at a later date. The only way this is possible is by credit cards where we can make minimum payments that enslave us for years or even decades. Most minimum payments on credit cards are only about 1% of the total balance each month, therefore making it affordable by dragging payments out. As we discussed, the interest on credit cards can compound if left on there and only minimum payments are made.

Many companies offer 0% financing for 2 to 3 years on televisions, cell phones, and other electronics, which allow us to make payments on items that we would not be able to afford, otherwise. This can be a great tool if you manage to pay it off in the allotted time and need the item to be productive, but oftentimes it is not repaid in time and accrues usury levels of interest.

Credit cards can be great if people use them to defer payments for up to 30 days and also earn reward points or cashback on some accounts. The key here is being responsible and paying these accounts in full each month so that no interest is incurred. I utilize mostly cash for my normal daily expenses because I can track it better and do not fall into the trap of a running balance on a credit card. If I do use my rewards cards for purchases, I ensure to budget for the amount and pay it off before interest is added to the account.

If you find yourself submerged in credit card debt, it is usually wise to pay down the card with the highest interest rate first and then work on the other debts in order. Although, some financial advisors may recommend paying off the lowest debt amount in full and then snowball payments to the next higher debt.

It is important to look at your situation and be creative and dedicated to correcting the situation. Dave Ramsey is a financial advisor who specializes in getting out of debt and could be a good resource if you want to create a game plan to attack your debt efficiently and stay out of debt.

It is also possible to call your card companies and ask for a lower or promotional rate. You may be surprised to see that they work with you on the terms or the fees that they charge. The most important thing is to assess where you currently are and create a plan to get out of debt.

Types of Business Credit

Just like consumer credit accounts, there can be many different creative products that you may be offered for your business. We will go over the basics and give you an idea of how you can get started or grow your business with the following credit accounts.

The first and easiest type of credit to get extended is a **business credit card** or local merchant account. I originally applied for a business credit card through a local bank, along with getting a business account with Lowe's and Staples. Over the years my account limits have increased as I have proven to be responsible.

This is how I started out building my different business credit profiles and is probably guaranteed by your personal credit in the early years. While I realize that it is important to separate yourself from the business, sometimes you may have to guarantee the accounts when starting out and until the business can start showing steady income and creditworthiness.

The second option is a **secured line of credit** or loan. Any secured loan or line of credit will require you to put up some form of collateral, or item(s) of value. Some examples of this may be business assets, real estate, or personal assets such as an individual retirement account or bank accounts. This usually will give you a lower interest rate on the loan because it is secured by something of value that can be collected if you do not pay the loan.

The next type is an **unsecured line of credit** or loan. With this type, you do not put up any collateral but they can be more difficult to grasp, especially with little experience. Most of the time they want to see that you have some business experience or have an established income stream within the business you are seeking financing. All you can do is know your business, be confident, and ask. The worst that can happen is you get a no. Eventually, you will become better at proposals and get a loan for the upgrades in your business. The interest rate on these accounts also tends to be a little higher because it is not secured by something of value.

The fourth type is a **real estate loan or line of credit**. These can be called Home Equity Lines of Credit (HELOC) and home equity loans. Essentially, you take equity from a piece of real estate that you own and use it to fund a business, investing, etc. These can be great, just pay attention to the terms of the loan and if it is a fixed or variable rate, and how much your payment will be each month. With these types of loans there are closing costs associated because there will be a note recorded with the real estate deed, so be sure to ask about the fees and associated costs. This is probably a good option for a larger loan and not so great for a small amount because of the fees associated with closing.

A final option is **venture capital or crowdfunding loans**. This type of business funding can be done mostly online with resources such as WeFunder, Kickstarter, PeerRealty, MicroVentures, and Crowdfunder, and more. Most things in business are negotiable and you can offer slices of equity and shop interest rates on different types of loans. These could be viable options depending on how you wanted to structure the deal.

I'm sure there are many other creative ways if you are willing to think outside the box. It all depends on how motivated you are when taking steps to turn your vision into reality. The main things to be aware of are the monthly recurring payment, associated fees, interest rate, amount of repayment time, personal liability or non-recourse, and equity shares.

CHAPTER 4
ASSETS & LIABILITIES

I prefer the way Robert Kiyosaki has put it so simply in the past, **"An asset puts money in your pocket while a liability takes money out of your pocket."** How can this concept be so simple, yet most consistently purchase liabilities instead of assets?

Many people find that they spend a majority of their money on liabilities and not on assets that make them additional income each month. Common liabilities include the new car in the garage, boats, motorcycles, big-screen televisions, the latest phones, and anything else that costs each month.

This is contrary to what most people will tell you and they believe their various toys are assets. If it doesn't produce income or a capital gain in the future, it is a liability. Look around your life and think about the things that increase your monthly income or deduct from your monthly income.

The concept of financial freedom is much more important to me than just acquiring a bunch of stuff. I have adjusted to a simple way of life where I realize that I do not need much to be satisfied. A lot of people called this a minimalistic lifestyle and I go through every six months to de-clutter my life.

Financial freedom is the idea that you can do as you choose from investments financing your lifestyle. It's as simple as having enough income coming in to cover all of your expenses and still have some leftover for future growth. The first step is to figure out all of your expenses to arrive at the minimum number that you need to create monthly.

If you need $3,000 per month to be financially free, you have to figure out what investments will generate that. Generally, the more you spend, the longer it will take to be financially free. That is another reason I live a simple life and do not crave most items that many people go for. I know this is a very different perspective than saving your way to retirement but in my opinion, it is much more efficient. It can be a slow process as you learn and build your portfolio but it is powerful and compounds over time.

I find multifamily rental properties a valuable resource to achieve that, along with service-oriented businesses, such as property management. I am a proponent of delayed gratification and investing time today to achieve what you want in the future.

What assets will you own to finance the lifestyle of your dreams? What liabilities can you get rid of so you have more room to purchase assets that give you freedom? You must sit down and think, along with asking challenging questions if you want to get out of your current situation.

How to Use Credit to purchase Assets & Liabilities

We have discussed a fair amount about credit and the different types of accounts that are readily available in the market. It is a two-edged sword that can be used to put you in a better or worse financial situation, depending on your understanding and your ability to utilize credit for assets and liabilities. **You can either use credit to purchase liabilities that cost you each month or you can use credit to purchase assets that will yield income each month.** If you want to be wealthy, it is extremely important to understand the concepts of using credit to leverage assets that generate income each month.

For example, if you take a loan to purchase business assets such as computers, a webpage, and marketing that yields a profit after you pay your loan, that is an example of taking on debt for assets. Another example is purchasing a rental duplex that provides $150 a month in income and a free place to live.

Debt for liabilities is taken on items such as a jet ski, vacation, and other luxuries that cost you money each month. I am not saying to tell the family you aren't going to the beach this year; I am simply saying don't spend the next three years financing it. If you want to purchase items or experiences you can save up and pay cash for them or have one of your assets make the monthly payment on them.

If you are financially responsible you can have a nice balance in both worlds and everything you desire. The person who is most diligent with their time and resources will be the first one to get off the financial hamster wheel. The question is: "What is most important to you right now?"

What is Equity & Net Worth?

Equity and net worth can be described as the result of assets minus liabilities. They are very similar in definition and equity usually concerns one particular interest in a property or a company, while net worth will describe the overall worth of an individual or company.

For example, if you own a house that is worth $100k and your mortgage balance is only $50k, then you have $50k equity in that home. You may also have a few more homes, a car, savings accounts, and a 401k that would contribute to your overall net worth. Equity refers to a specific item while net worth refers to an individual or company's total value.

If the value of the item you are financing is worth more than you owe, it is stated that you have positive equity in an item. Negative equity or being upside down is when you owe more on a credit account than the current market value.

In chapter 7, we will show you how to calculate your net worth and track it over time. Watching your equity and net worth grow takes discipline, patience, and continuous effort toward purchasing assets that grow in value.

CHAPTER 5
INCOME & EXPENSES

Types of Income

The 3 types of income are **earned, portfolio, and passive**. **Earned income** is also known as active or ordinary income and is derived from wages, salaries, and tips from your employer or self-employment. It is the highest taxed income, especially if you are a high earner. This is income that you only receive by being active such as going to your job each day.

The tax system is progressive and charges you more as your taxable income increases. Depending on how much you make, there can be a federal income tax between 10 to 37%. Your income is also subject to 7.65% for Social Security & Medicare taxes, and state income tax, if applicable. We will break down the rates further in the tax section ahead.

This is the highest percentage of income received in most parts of the World. Income derived from employment can be a stable and valuable source that you can invest to gain portfolio or passive income but it's important to understand that earned income is the highest taxed, making it less efficient than the rest.

The next type is **portfolio income** and this is income or gains derived from investments. The interest income you make from savings, CDs, Money Market, or loans are good examples of this income. Dividends from stocks or an ETF that is held in a non-retirement account is another example. Each account that accrues interest or dividends will send you a 1099 annually that shows the gains.

In addition to interest or dividend income, the other example of portfolio income is called a capital gain. A **capital gain** is any profit over the cost of the investment. Selling cryptocurrencies, real estate, stocks, or commodities for a profit is a good example of this. It is broken down into short-term and long-term capital gains by the IRS for tax purposes.

If you hold an investment longer than one year and sell it is considered long-term capital gains and taxed between 0% and 20%, based on your tax bracket.

If you sell an investment within one year, you are taxed on the gain at your ordinary tax rate (the same federal tax rate you pay on your earned income). However, no portfolio gain is subject to Social Security or Medicare payroll taxes, which saves you 7.65% when compared to earned income.

The 3rd type of income is **passive income.** This is income where you put in work upfront and reap the financial rewards at a later date. Imagine being a farmer and planting seeds for the future. You will have to water it for growth but as long as the climate remains stable it will produce in abundance.

What can you do today where the value in the future grows? How can you create sustainable monthly income, managed by systems, that you aren't actively involved in? The idea here is that you cannot be active in day-to-day activities and is more like an automated system that generates income.

For example, I have hundreds of hours researching information and writing this book. I realize this is active at the time but will yield passive income through royalties at a later date. I also invest in multifamily units to lease out and provide affordable housing. These are just two examples where the income derived is passive (not derived from my day-to-day activities) and taxed at a lower rate than earned income.

With real estate rentals, you can depreciate the building and spend qualified amounts in the business which reduces your tax liability further. I encourage real estate because it has a lot of tax advantages, especially as a rental owner and passive partner.

The key is to find income that is efficient and flows to you with the least amount of resistance. Consult with a Certified Public Accountant (CPA) on creating tax-efficient income sources. Do you want to trade away all of your time for earned income or cultivate resources that generate more efficient income?

Types of Expenses

The 4 types of expenses are **Variable, Fixed, Intermittent,** and **Discretionary**.

Variable expenses can be described as expenses that are recurring but fluctuate each month. Think about your electricity and water expenses. The more of these that you use, the higher the expense will be. You can reduce these by consuming less. Taxes are another example of a variable expense because they change depending on your income.

Fixed expenses are set recurring expenses such as your rent, student loans, or auto loans. They are the same each month forever or until the debt is extinguished. You can reduce these by paying them off or exchange an expensive payment item for a cheaper alternative. Even if you just make extra payments toward the principal of these fixed loans, you can drastically reduce the overall interest paid and free up cash to put toward investment.

Intermittent expenses are those costs that are unexpected such as a car or home repair. It is important to have an emergency fund set up to cover these intermittent expenses that seem to come at inopportune times.

The last and most manageable are **discretionary expenses** which can be described as wants rather than needs. Examples are dining out at restaurants, gifts, and entertainment. We always have command over this category and once we take control it will allow us to keep more of our income, pay off debt, and invest more. Start with these expenses when you analyze your budget and you will quickly see how much you spend each month and how to reduce them.

Where do you have a leak with expenses and how can you reduce these to keep more in your pocket? I like to keep total expenses around 40% or less of gross income and invest the rest through a specific allocation, that I will show you in Chapter 9. I think you will find that most wealthy people live off of a small portion of their income while multiplying the rest through wise investment strategies over time.

This will probably be challenging to do at first but is very possible with a little hard work and determination. If you can do better than that, you will increase your speed on the road to financial freedom.

What is Net Income?

Net income is the number that you have remaining each month after you subtract all of your allotments and expenses from your income. Hopefully, this number is positive or equals zero if you are using a zero-based budget and have allocated wisely to investing and saving.

One issue that I notice is that as people's income increases over time, so do their expenses. They take on larger liabilities, such as more expensive cars and homes, while never gaining any long-term benefits from income increases. It's a perpetual cycle that keeps us from getting off the financial hamster wheel. You have to choose if you want to be wealthy or just appear rich and keep up with the neighbors.

As we stated earlier, the goal is to purchase assets that increase your income. Most people first have to take control of their earned income from their jobs or current businesses before they can grow their portfolio or passive income from investing. This can be done by reducing expenses and taxes then increasing amounts dedicated to investing. The challenging part is taking responsibility and looking at your current situation through the income statement and balance sheet in chapter 7.

Even if you only have one income stream right now, you must keep expenses reasonable, so you have some leftover for savings and investment. Without first taking charge of your income and expenses, you will never be able to execute the more advanced strategies of building wealth.

CHAPTER 6
TAXES

Federal Personal Income Tax

Most of us know that taxes will usually be our biggest expense as long as we are employees and/or business owners in the US. Did you know as an American you are subject to worldwide taxation unless you meet certain criteria? You are also required to file tax returns by April 15th if you earned more than the standard deduction the previous year. The IRS is the regulating authority for collecting tax payments for the US Treasury and they can impose fines or even imprisonment if you do not play by their rules.

Gross income is the total amount of income you have made during the year. The current tax code allows for certain exemptions and deductions from this number to arrive at taxable income. Currently, for single people, the standard deduction is $12,400 which will reduce your gross income by that amount. If you are married, the standard deduction doubles. Many other exemptions and deductions may apply to you at **www.irs.gov**.

The IRS takes that taxable income and divides it into blocks of income for tax at a progressive rate. For example, the first $9,875 you earn will be taxed at 10%, while the next block of income from $9,876 to $40,125 will be taxed at 12%. These are called marginal tax rates. Once you multiply each marginal tax rate to each block of income and total them, you will arrive at your current tax liability for the year.

If you take the total amount owed and divide that by your gross income you will get the federal effective tax rate. This is the overall percentage that the federal government took from you that year to run its operations. Keep in mind, this is just the amount that goes to the federal government and we will discuss the other payroll taxes and state taxes below.

If you are **self-employed**, also known as a sole proprietor, you will pay 15.3% of your income up to $137,700 to self-employment tax. This breaks down to 12.4% going to Social Security and 2.9% for Medicare. Essentially, you are paying the employee and employer portion of the payroll taxes that subsidize the elderly population with healthcare and retirement income. In addition to this self-employment tax, you will pay the appropriate amount of federal income tax based on your salary.

One benefit of being self-employed is that you can deduct half of the self-employment taxes because you are acting as the employer, along with deducting business expenses to reduce your overall tax liability. This helps to keep more in your pocket throughout the year. As you will see in the business section below, being able to spend on qualified business expenses reduces your tax liability and is more efficient than being taxed at payroll and using what is left over.

Business Income

There are many different business entities today, so the first thing is to understand business formation and the tax implications of each. For starters, there are Corporations, Limited Liability Companies, and Partnerships. In an attempt to keep this simple, I will recommend speaking to a qualified CPA, review business formation at **investopedia.com,** and read tax laws on **irs.gov**.

The main tax benefit of a business, when compared to an employee, is the number of deductions that they are allowed and the net tax liability. When you bring in business income, you can then spend some of that on qualifying business expenses such as advertising, business interest, office rent, travel expenses, insurance, equipment, inventory, and much more.

After these expenses, you are left with a much lower number that is taxable but you have usually created more value in the business if you have spent wisely. You also have control over the capital until you pay the quarterly or annual taxes, which can further grow through interest or investment. Being able to spend money and taxed on the remainder seems much more efficient than taxed immediately at payroll as an employee. You can look up all eligible business deductions at **www.irs.gov/businesses**

Payroll Taxes

One of the next higher taxes after federal income tax comes from our payroll as an employee or business owner. Social Security takes 6.2% of your paycheck to provide retirement income to those over age 62, who qualify. According to the Social Security Administration, Social Security will have to reduce payouts as early as 2035 by 20%, if they do not pass legislation to make changes to this program.

Medicare is the payroll tax that subsidizes healthcare costs for those over 65 and younger people with disabilities. 1.45% of your paycheck goes to funding this program. We will discuss both of these in more detail in the retirement section.

State Taxes

43 of the 50 states have a form of state income tax that ranges from 1% to 12.3%, dependent upon your income and location. 7 states do not have an income tax and those are Alaska, Florida, Nevada, South Dakota, Texas, Washington, and Wyoming. This is something you always have control over and a way you can reduce your tax liability and enjoy where you live.

The next most important tax to consider when looking at states to live within is property taxes. This will not affect you if you choose to lease items such as a car or house but mostly affects those who want to own a primary residence, rental property, or other property such as a car, boat, motorcycle, etc.

Property tax for real estate owned averages 1% of the property value but can go higher than 2.5%, depending on location and ownership status. Investment real estate usually has higher property taxes than primary residences. All states have this property tax on real estate, while 27 states charge additional annual property taxes on vehicles, boats, motorcycles, and other property. Be sure to look at annual taxes on property if you plan to own a lot.

Sales taxes are charged for most sales in 45 out of the 50 states. There can also be a local municipality tax in addition to the statewide sales tax on transactions. The 5 states that do not have a statewide sales tax are Alaska, Delaware, Montana, New Hampshire, and Oregon. This is a much lower tax when compared to a state income or property tax, so I rank this much lower when looking at places to live.

Ways to Reduce Taxes

The tax code is ever-changing and can be difficult to understand. I have tried to simplify an overview and hopefully shed light on how we can keep more of our income. I recommend seeking a qualified CPA and become familiar with tax laws that can be used to your benefit.

As we can see above, **finding the right state to live in can drastically reduce state tax on your income, property taxes on the property held, and the sales tax on goods purchased or sold**. I like the idea of living in one of the states that do not have a state income tax or at minimum a lower state income tax with reasonable property taxes.

My current home location is Florida so I pay no state income tax and the rental properties are located in South Carolina, where property taxes are reasonable. Imagine keeping an additional 5% to 10% of your income just based on where you live! With the technological changes in employment and opportunity, you are no longer restricted to living where you grew up and can venture out to see which places may be a better fit for yourself and your family.

If you sell the primary residence that you have lived in for the previous 2 out of 5 years, you may be eligible to exclude up to $250,000 of the gain from taxes. This doubles if you are married and can be a valuable bit of information if you move often and seem to live in appreciating areas. If you do not fit in this criterion, it can cost you up to 20% of the gain in taxes, so it is important to be familiar with the basics of tax law or hire someone who is. **www.irs.gov**

A **1031 exchange** is a swap of investment property for another that allows capital gains taxes to be deferred. At the time of this writing, the new investment(s) must be identified within 45 days and transferred within 180 days. Be sure to consult with your CPA and find a Qualified Intermediary to handle the transaction.

www.irs.gov/businesses/small-businesses-self-employed/like-kind-exchanges-real-estate-tax-tips

Contributing to a tax-deferred retirement account such as the 401k, IRA, or life insurance policy can reduce your current tax liability, especially if you are a high earner. Of course, it is important to create a plan for the future taxes due but there are several investments where you can postpone taxes with the proper contributions.

www.thebalance.com/how-do-401k-tax-deductions-work-4159586

In addition to your investment accounts, you can also **contribute to your children's education accounts** and setting them up for success. This will reduce your current tax liability while saving the proceeds for education costs that your child could incur in the future.

There are systems in the tax code that allow you to **work outside the US for 330 days or more in a 12-month period to exclude $105,900 of your income.** This amount increases annually for inflation. For those people who are travel seekers and looking to dramatically increase their net income, this is a great resource to keep a majority of that currency you earn.

https://www.irs.gov/individuals/international-taxpayers/foreign-earned-income-exclusion

Tax advantageous locations do not charge tax on capital gains or Social Security. Puerto Rico and Belize are just two examples of locations that offer lower taxes to incentivize business activities and investment. Doing some research on tax-advantageous countries might give you the inspiration to open a business elsewhere and create a new love for where you live. Do a search for opportunity zones in your local area or different parts of the world that interest you.

The business tax code differs drastically from the employee system that most people fall within. **Even if you start a side business it is possible to reduce your tax liability**. Maybe you will qualify to use a portion of your primary residence as a home office or deduct a portion of the car payment when you utilize it in business. There are so many deductions on the IRS website for you to utilize beneficially.

https://www.irs.gov/businesses/small-businesses-self-employed/deducting-business-expenses

Charitable contributions can be tax-deductible and they don't even have to be in cash. Perhaps you have donated clothes, food, household items, or more to a local charity. Be sure to get a receipt from the charity for accounting purposes.

https://www.irs.gov/forms-pubs/about-publication-526

Overall, there are many ways to reduce your tax liability each year that fit neatly within the confines of the IRS tax code. I am just scratching the surface on ideas to reduce taxes and you owe it to yourself to become more efficient.

PART II:
HOW TO TAKE CONTROL

CHAPTER 7
FINANCIAL STATEMENTS

What is a Financial Statement?

A financial statement is an actual financial record of an organization or individual. They can be used to measure where you currently are and to track progress over time. The two financial statements that we will discuss are called the income statement and the balance sheet.

The **income statement** shows your income sources, allocates amounts for saving, investing, and giving while deducting all other expenses to arrive at net income. We will focus on allocating our income efficiently and increasing the percentages dedicated to saving and investing, over time.

The **balance sheet** shows what you own and owe at the current time while calculating the difference. Assets are what you own, liabilities are what you owe, and net worth is the difference.

As you increase your income on the income statement, the goal is to invest in real assets that will increase your net worth on the balance sheet. Over time, as you increase assets on the balance sheet, they should show up on your income statement as business income, dividends, interest, royalties, real estate income, or capital gains.

For example, if we build a business that sells t-shirts online, it may generate $100 per month of business income on the income statement. We may sell stock from our balance sheet that would create a capital gain on the income statement. We may rent a duplex that adds $300 of real estate income to the left side of our income statement. At that point, we will redirect this income into the investment that makes the most sense at the time.

I have included the editable "Freedom Spreadsheet" excel link in the back of the book, so you can update and track your growth each pay period. This is the same income statement and balance sheet I use to track growth and is necessary if you want to take your finances to the next level.

Income Statement

We will start with the income statement which shows the income coming in and how we allocated the resources that month. We will forecast numbers in the budget column for the current month and will record actual data at the end of the month to see how we did. This is the bedrock for wealth creation and is imperative to your success.

INCOME STATEMENT

Income		Allotments & Expenses			
SOURCE	**AMOUNT**	**ALLOTMENTS**	**BUDGET**	**ACTUAL**	**% OF GROSS INCOME**
Salary:	$ 5,200.00	Saving:	$ 750.00	$ 800.00	14%
Business:	$ 100.00	Investing:	$ 1,000.00	$ 1,100.00	20%
Interest:	$ 3.00	Giving:	$ 160.00	$ 125.00	2%
Dividends:	$ 8.00				
Royalties:	$ 25.00				
Real Estate:	$ 275.00	**EXPENSES**	**BUDGET**	**ACTUAL**	**% OF GROSS INCOME**
Capital Gain:	$ 25.00	Taxes	$ 800.00	$ 813.00	14%
		Housing	$ 985.00	$ 985.00	17%
		Utilities	$ 150.00	$ 133.00	2%
		Food	$ 400.00	$ 392.00	7%
		Vehicle	$ 310.00	$ 310.00	6%
		Fuel	$ 75.00	$ 60.00	1%
		Insurance	$ 130.00	$ 130.00	2%
		Entertainment	$ -	$ 25.00	0%
		Clothing	$ -	$ 48.00	1%
		Medical	$ 50.00	$ 50.00	1%
		Debt Payments	$ 96.00	$ 110.00	2%
		School/Child Care	$ 275.00	$ 275.00	5%
		Vacation	$ 100.00	$ 100.00	2%
		Misc.	$ 355.00	$ 180.00	3%
GROSS INCOME	**$ 5,636.00**	**TOTAL EXPENSES**	**$ 3,726.00**	**$ 3,611.00**	64%
		NET INCOME	$ -	$ -	

The numbers on the left are your income sources while the right side is for allotments and expenses. The net income number at the bottom is the difference between the two. I like to get this net income to zero because that means we have allocated each dollar to a specific destination. This is often referred to as a zero-based budget and ensures that you are directing your money efficiently.

Most people will have a salary or earned income from their jobs or businesses that will go on the first line. The next few lines are for other income sources and ones we want to increase through businesses, interest, dividends, royalties, real estate, and other capital gains. This is the income that can eventually replace your earned income.

As we move to the right side you notice something interesting; First, there are allotments for saving, investing, and giving. I believe in paying yourself first and establishing the important percentages, upfront.

Once you establish these standards, then we make deductions by labeling our normal monthly expenses, such as taxes, housing, utilities, food, vehicle, insurance, etc. Be sure to account for all of your expenses during this exercise so that you aren't left with any surprises. It's a good idea to leave an allowance in the Misc. category for any unexpected expenses that may arise that month. This is necessary especially before you get your emergency reserves established.

I have input the formulas so the spreadsheet will calculate percentages of your gross income that are allotted for saving, investing, and giving. It also calculates percentages for specific expenses such as taxes, food, entertainment, child care, housing, and more. If you do not have access to a computer you can always calculate your percentages and final numbers manually by using the book image as a reference. This will help you see where most of your cash is going and assist with making changes along the way.

As you reduce expenses over time it will allow more funds to be set aside for debt paydown, saving, and investing. It is important to pay attention to how much you are spending if you want to multiply some through investing.

If we have done a great job at the end of the month there should be zero or a positive net income. If we have created a positive at the end of the month, we can contribute to additional debt reduction, savings, business/investments, charity, or choose to splurge into some of the discretionary expenses that we want.

It's not until we take account that we truly understand our current situation and what we need to do to change it. We will update this monthly to show actual data and compare our progress over time.

Balance Sheet

Now, you should have a plan established on where to cut expenses and increase income through the income statement. Our next focus will be creating a balance sheet that will show your current net worth and allow you to track your growth. A balance sheet shows your total assets on the left side with liabilities on the right and hopefully a positive net worth number at the bottom right.

Assets-Liabilities=Net Worth.

When I decided to take my finances seriously, I was $5,000 in credit card debt with maybe $2,000 in savings after a dramatic injury that left me out of work for six months. Don't beat yourself up if you find you are in a difficult situation; use this as the time to understand where you are financially and create a plan to move in the right direction.

List all assets such as your home, vehicles, cash, bank accounts, retirement accounts, jewelry, firearms, electronics, metals, etc. and we can make adjustments along the way. The key in time is to differentiate real assets, perceived assets, and liabilities to make smarter decisions in the future.

BALANCE SHEET

REAL ASSETS	MARKET VALUE	% of Net Worth	LIABILITIES	AMT OWED
Cash on Hand:	$ 800.00	1%	Home Mortgage:	$ 100,000.00
Bank Accounts:	$ 6,500.00	4%	Home Equity Line:	$ 7,200.00
Retirement Account (401k, 403b, etc.):	$ 23,560.00	16%	Property Mortgages:	$ 200,000.00
ROTH and/or Pre Tax IRA:	$ 1,100.00	1%	Business Loans:	
Mutual Funds:		0%	Vehicle Loans:	
Cryptocurrency:	$ 4,000.00	3%	Credit Cards:	$ 350.00
Stocks, ETF's, REIT's (Taxable Acct):	$ 3,500.00	2%	Student Loans:	$ 12,000.00
Real Estate:	$ 239,000.00	26%	Personal Loans:	
Business Equipment:	$ 3,000.00	2%	Other Loans:	
Precious Metals, Commodities:	$ 4,000.00	3%		
Life Insurance Cash Value:	$ -	0%		
Annuities:	$ -	0%		

PERCEIVED ASSETS	MARKET VALUE	% of Net Worth
Vehicles:	$ 9,200.00	6%
House:	$ 165,000.00	39%
Jewelry:	$ 300.00	0%
Furniture:	$ 5,000.00	3%
Clothing:	$ 500.00	0%
Personal Belongings:	$ 2,000.00	1%
TOTAL ASSETS	**$ 467,460.00**	

TOTAL LIABILITIES	**$ 319,550.00**

NET WORTH: Total Assets - Liabilities =	**$ 147,910.00**

Next, you are going to subtract any liabilities on the right side, such as your mortgage, car loan, credit card debt, student loans, etc. All the debt that you currently have will be liabilities. This is going to be an eye-opener for most people and we can understand how we got into the current situation with the liabilities we have taken on.

Understand this is common with the system we live in, especially in America. Most people are way overleveraged but you must take the steps to put it in check and make sacrifices to get out of the situation. Let the spreadsheet do all the heavy lifting as I have input the formulas to total the assets, liabilities, and finalize a net worth figure.

Finally, we have a net worth number that is real and we can track over time that will give us a progress report for how we are managing our finances. I like to look at the income statement and balance sheet every two weeks to make sure I stay on track with the goals I have set. Updating these spreadsheets on your computer each payday will be a good place to start as you build a new habit. On average, it takes 66 days to form a habit so stay diligent with tracking and making smarter financial choices over time.

Look at the templates I have provided and use them as a guide if you don't understand something. I realize that these sheets can be difficult to understand if you have never seen them before but are the standard for financial intelligence.

Over time, as we make wise decisions with investments and get rid of liabilities, we will see our income increase and our net worth grow. I strive to see my net worth grow each month because that indicates I have increased assets. I also like to see my income grow over time as I increase my business, real estate, and other investment income.

If you see your net worth or income go backward, you usually have made a poor financial choice and need to make some corrections. The income statement and balance sheet become easier to track with practice and let you know if you are making better or worse financial decisions, over time.

STOP NOW before you read any further and take the time to fill out the income statement and balance sheet. These are the first steps to understanding where you are and how you can make your situation better. Without taking these first steps, the future subjects will not be as effective for you.

CHAPTER 8
SAVINGS & RETIREMENT

The basics of savings have been around for ages and have been a prudent concept for those that wanted to store value for the future. It is delayed gratification that will allow you to do as you desire at a later date. As we learned in Chapter 2, for many years gold and silver have been used as money, but that is no longer the case.

Since 1971, we have a fiat currency that is backed solely by the belief in the value, which governments decide. As central banks continuously expand the currency, we are losing the purchasing power of our current dollars through inflation.

With knowing this, I do not think it is smart to save cash the way our elders saved money. When they saved money, it was a stable account of value and didn't lose purchasing power the way our currency does today.

To combat emergencies and downtimes in our economy I believe it is intelligent to create reserves equaling 6 months of our current expenses. No matter how great your life is there will always be times when challenging things happen and it costs you money. This may take some time to create but you can do it with the income statement and taking charge of each dollar you receive. Notice I call them reserves and do not believe in massive savings that sit there and earn little to no interest.

After reserves, we also have to accumulate cash for down payments on our business ideas, real estate, or purchasing other investments. Without some reserves and funds ready for investment you won't get very far. I use the income statement monthly to track where my money goes and also have a few productive habits to allocate funds for investing:

I set up a transfer to go to a separate saving or investment account every week. This way I am not tempted to spend it and I realize I would have to steal it from my investment accounts to utilize it. It's the idea of paying yourself first because most people will increase their expenses to meet or exceed their income.

I habitually do the transfers through my online banking app, which makes it very easy. I also keep a list of bills with due dates and go into mobile banking bi-weekly to electronically pay the appropriate companies. This takes me around 20 minutes and is critical in the way I save for investments and make payments on time, which has led to an excellent credit score.

I leave just enough in my checking account to cover the bills that will come out that week, along with the weekly allowance I get from the ATM to cover food, fuel, entertainment, and a $100 cushion for anything unexpected. Think back to that zero-based budget that we discussed.

I have overdraft protection linked to a credit card for anything that could overdraw my checking account. Everything else gets transferred immediately to my investment accounts for growth. If you get paid bi-weekly or monthly, you can use the same recipe, just tweak it for your pay period.

Taking cash out weekly for typical expenses during the week helps me keep track of what I spend and responsible for it because I know the amount is limited. Let's say I take out $200 for the week to eat at restaurants, gas, and anything else. Once that cash is gone, I do not go get more so it makes me very aware of what I am spending and how much I have remaining for the week. It's another level of accountability. If you do not spend the full allowance one week, you can save it in cash or splurge another week.

In addition to the cash allowance, when I got serious with finances, I would write down every dime I spent in a notebook and it made me extremely aware of what I was spending money on and where I could cut costs. Also, if I want to purchase a big expense item, I will sleep on the idea for 24 hours and see if it is still important to me then.

I currently use the "Freedom Spreadsheet" for tracking finances and still use the cash allowance for daily expenses and an alternate way to pay in case credit cards or digital wallets aren't working.

I have reserves that cover all of my personal and business expenses for six months; I keep these in a separate savings account that I never touch. This allows me to remain calm during times of uncertainty and think clearly about how to make the situation better when issues arise.

The only logical thing I see to do with the rest of the currency after establishing reserves is to invest in a plan that will multiply the amount over time. If we aren't making at least a 2% return each year, we are losing purchasing power. That is the average reported rate of inflation and the real rate could be much higher. We will discuss investments in the next chapter so we can understand how to minimize losses to inflation.

Retirement

Another common reason people save is to one day stop working and retire. The standard system that we see, tells us we should work most of our lives while saving and investing in mostly indexed mutual funds and bonds, and then at retirement, we can stop working and finally enjoy some of our life. According to Money Magazine, the average retirement age is 62. I don't know about you but I don't want to invest strictly in assets that I have minimal control over and wait that long in the process...

This seems to be a backward concept to me. Why would we work most of our lives away and then try to enjoy some of it when we are elderly and have lost our youth? I realize we need to have the capital to do things such as exploring Italy and gambling in Las Vegas; but if we budget accordingly and make smart investments early, we can do many of the great things that retirement has to offer while we are still young. Even if you are middle-aged it's possible to make the adjustments needed through the income statement and balance sheet.

We will discuss the more traditional paths to retirement from conventional wisdom and then get into what many consider to be more efficient.

Government Subsidized Retirement

Let's start with **Social Security** as most people know of this system. It is subsidized retirement income paid out to individuals or their spouses who have contributed to the system for a minimum of 10 years and are at least the age of 62. If you are disabled and younger than that age, you may be eligible for Social Security by visiting the link below:

www.ssa.gov/ssi/text-eligibility-ussi.htm

The Social Security system is funded by taking 6.2% of current employee paychecks and a matching 6.2% from their employer to transfer to current retirees. In years past, there was a surplus of taxes brought in but now there is not enough to transfer directly to current retirees. For years, these surpluses would go into a trust fund that bought US Treasuries and grew over time. From 1982 until 2018, the fund received a surplus that gained interest from these Treasury investments. However, since 2018 its payouts to retirees are now more than it takes in through taxation.

In 1960, 5.1 individuals were paying into Social Security for every person withdrawing from it. As of 2020, only 2.6 individuals are paying into the program, according to the Board of Trustees of the Federal Old-Age and Survivors Insurance Trust Fund. People are also living many years longer than in times past, which contributes to the shortage of funds. It is pretty easy to see what is happening to this fund and where it may be in the future.

The full retirement age to receive benefits is age 67, but you can early retire and start receiving payments at age 62. If you decide to take the payments earlier at 62, the payments are reduced and you will receive about 70% of what you would at age 67.

The amount you receive depends on the amounts that you have paid in but is said to supply approximately 40% of your normal working income. Depending on your income level at retirement, your Social Security income can be taxed. For example, if you are married and make over $44,000 of provisional income currently, up to 85% of the Social Security income is taxable.

It is important to speak with a competent CPA to ensure your retirement is set up with minimal tax liability and the proper investments that will yield the desired income. There is a great book called "The Power of Zero" by David McKnight that explains retirement taxation and plans to be tax efficient.

As time goes on and lesser people pay into this system, I see the benefit amounts being reduced, and possibly all of the income received will be taxable. The official report from the Social Security Administration states that they will have to reduce benefits as early as 2035 by 20%. You can go to **www.ssa.gov** to input your personal information and see how much you have paid and how much you may receive at retirement.

Medicare is a subsidized medical coverage that some people consider part of their retirement. This entitlement is funded by the government taking 1.45% of each current employee's paycheck and a matching amount from the employer. Medicare provides subsidized medical care when you or your spouse have paid into the system for 10 years and reach the age of 65. If you are disabled and younger than that age, you may be eligible for Medicare by checking the link below:

www.medicare.gov/eligibilitypremiumcalc

Pensions – Defined Benefit Plans

Currently, only around 13% of American workers have a pension plan that will pay guaranteed income when they retire. This is an older system and mostly applies to government or state employees today. Although, there are still some larger corporations such as UPS, Coca-Cola, ExxonMobil, and others that offer pension plans.

Pensions were a common retirement system offered in America until around 1978 but have declined rapidly since the introduction of the Revenue Act of 1978. Up until then, around 45% of Americans had a pension plan that would pay them guaranteed income for the duration of their lives, upon retirement.

The Revenue Act of 1978 amended the IRS code, section 401(k) allowing individuals to start creating retirement plans in addition to their pensions. This legislation seemed to shift the responsibility of retirement and guaranteed income for life from the employer to the employee. Now, most people have to organize their retirement through a 401(k) or similar plan over time. I believe this is one reason why having a basic understanding of personal finance is so important today if we ever want to gain financial freedom.

If you do have a pension, you can look up your specific state, federal, or corporate pension plans to gain more details on amounts and what you may receive at retirement age. This is your retirement and is important to know so make sure to speak with the proper department in your organization. You may also be able to do some research at the Pension Benefit Guaranty Corporation: **www.pbgc.gov/**

IRA's and 401(k)'s – Defined Contribution Plans

IRA's and 401k's are the most common retirement plans that you will hear about today. Think of these as tax-free or tax-deferred housing for investments that are kept inside. The two are similar in the fact that they are both retirement plans, but the 401k is employer-created, while an Individual Retirement Account (IRA) is individually created. We will discuss some of the investments within these plans in the Investments section.

You can self-manage these plans or hire managers to look after them. Take time to learn the basics of these plans, the fees, and consult with a qualified accountant that can help you understand the outcomes for traditional, after-tax, and ROTH plans.

I like to ask advisors what they invest in and the standing of their portfolio if they are going to be advising me on my retirement portfolio. Be sure the advisors take their own medicine and aren't just making a commission off of you. Birds of a feather tend to flock together so I prefer to seek counsel from individuals with integrity and that are financially savvy themselves. I self-manage my IRA with indexed ETFs, such as Vanguard Total Index Fund (VTI) to avoid these management fees while gaining steady growth in a diversified group of top-tier companies.

The traditional IRA or 401k is a tax-deferred account that allows you to input pretax dollars and be taxed at a later date when you withdraw at retirement, after 59 ½ years of age. You can withdraw any time after this age and are required to take distributions after 70 ½ years of age.

Contributions to a traditional IRA or 401k will reduce your tax liability for the current year because the dollars are input before being taxed. These tax-deferred dollars get the benefit of growing until retirement distribution. Just remember that taxes will be due at retirement and that can be a substantial bill, so include this in your plan. It is highly recommended to let funds stay in until the retirement age of 59 ½ because the IRS may penalize you up to 10% of the proceeds, in addition to any taxes due, if you withdraw early.

If there comes a time where you need to access the cash, you may be eligible to take a loan up to 50% of your vested balance in the IRA or 401k. Be sure to check within your specific plan before you decide on a withdrawal. Loans are not considered taxable occurrences, so it may be a better solution.

This account type is premised around taxes not going up in the future and you taking smaller distributions during retirement which will be taxed lower than current income. I tend to disagree with this approach and again recommend reading "The Power of Zero" by David McKnight to study retirement distributions and taxes while discussing with a competent CPA.

The ROTH IRA or 401k is funded with after-tax dollars. This is a retirement option if you believe you will be in the same or higher tax bracket at retirement age. The idea here is to go ahead and pay tax now so you don't have to deal with it at retirement or potentially be taxed higher. All gains will grow tax-free as long as you make disbursements after age 59 ½; there are also no required minimum distributions on these accounts at age 70 ½.

Even if you withdraw your contributions early from a ROTH plan, provided that you have had the account active for five years, you are entitled to the contributions tax and penalty-free. If you wish to take the earnings out before retirement age, you will have to pay the appropriate taxes and penalties on these gains, just like a traditional plan.

Currently, you can contribute as much as $6,000 to an IRA, with an additional $1,000 if you are over 50. For 401k's, you can contribute as much as $19,500 with an additional $6,500 for those over 50.

Some employers will match a percentage of what you put into your 401k account that can help increase your balance. You may find that they will insert 50 cents for each dollar you deposit, up to a certain percentage. This usually ranges between 4% to 6% of your salary. I encourage contributing to a 401k plan, whether ROTH or traditional if your employer is willing to match. This is free capital and an instant increase in your net worth.

There is another option known as **Self-Directed IRA (SDIRA)**. These are designed for you to have more control over the investments and can range from stocks, bonds, mutual funds, ETFs, real estate, precious metals, and more. You may have full access to these accounts with a digital checkbook where it's possible to make investments of your choice that day.

All of these investments must be processed through your IRA custodian to be legal and non-taxable. Do some research on Self Directed IRAs and who may be a good custodian for you. The services and costs can vary drastically from different companies so be sure to get referrals and perform your due diligence.

These are the most common retirement plans available through your employer and financial planners today. However, you do not have to go the conventional route and can be as creative as you want to be. We will discuss options in the Investments section that can be housed in one of these retirement plans or purchased separately as you build your retirement portfolio.

Whatever route you decide to go, the key is to create a plan and start funding it for retirement. I have never met anyone in life that wishes they would have started later, but I hear often that most people wish they would have started earlier.

Retirement Concepts

Most financial planners will recommend that you fund an account that will provide around 80% of your pre-retirement income during retirement. The reason they propose the lower percentage of your income is because you should not require as much income in retirement due to paying off most of your debts, no more funds going toward your retirement accounts, and you automatically save 7.65% from Social Security and Medicare payroll tax, along with your needs being reduced.

While I agree that some of these variables may be true; I tend to disagree with this approach because if I am fully retired, I am sure I will spend more money than I would if I were going to work each day. A lot of people will be looking for things to keep them occupied that will cost more than they ordinarily would spend. I'm sure you can test this theory by taking the family on summer vacation and then checking account balances afterward.

Also, if this is the time you have been saving and working so hard for, why would you want to be cheap and not enjoy retirement? It has been shown that most people spend a lot more than they originally anticipated, especially during the first few years of retirement. I would plan to use the same 100% of pre-retirement income and if you have some leftover, it can be a cushion for the coming years or amounts to donate.

The average retirement age is 62 years old and they recommend planning for a minimum of 20 years after retirement. If you consider retiring at the average age of 62, a life expectancy of 20 years, with $50,000 per year being dispersed to you, that equates to a total account balance of $1 million needed. This is a basic example and needs to be adjusted for your specific scenario but gives you an idea of how conventional wisdom expects you to save your way to retirement.

There are some great calculators you can use that allow you to play with different variables such as age, monthly contributions, age of retirement, and rate of return on investments to plan for retirement. Check out **www.nerdwallet.com/investing** for a calculator that can be helpful for this. Most retirement calculators will use an average of 6% to 8% rate of return because that is considered to be the average annualized gain overtime in an indexed fund. Experimenting with retirement calculators and, your income statement, and balance sheet will help you get a better idea of where you currently are and how to get to where you need to be.

Now that we know the basics of retirement plans, how to fund them, and an estimate of what we will need to have at retirement age, we can think about how we might take disbursements in retirement. There are a few different concepts when taking distributions any time after age 59 ½.

Probably the most common method is the 4% rule, where you take a fixed 4% of everything you have accrued in your portfolio the first year and every year after. Another variant of the 4% rule recommends taking an additional 2% after the first year to keep up with inflation.

The third common option is what they call the bucket disbursement method. This is the idea that you have a diversified portfolio of cash, bonds, and stocks. Upon retirement, you will first use the cash to live on in retirement, while letting the other two buckets continue to grow through dividends and appreciation and feeding the cash bucket that you live off of. Over time, you will dip into the other buckets that make the most sense at the time that you need them. "How much Money do I Need to Retire" by Todd Tresidder explains retirement strategies, growth, and disbursements better.

We have shown you the basic concepts of traditional retirement plans and now we will discuss what some believe is an easier alternative. To me, saving your way to retirement is an inefficient way to fund your retirement. Why would you struggle each year to set aside currency that you place in the markets and have very little control over?

Wouldn't it be great if you could take those dollars that you set aside and put them into a business, partnership, or real estate, where you could see the fruits of your labors and growth over time? I realize that this idea is not for everybody and the reason I overviewed the traditional retirement information first.

However, I dare you to consider the idea of taking a chance on yourself in a business that you believe in, a partnership that yields dividends or interest, creating content for royalties, or leasing property for income. There are countless ideas but these are just a few that I have found to produce positive results. Instead of saving capital and investing only in paper assets, this is an alternate idea to fund retirement where you replace your employment income with sustainable and recurring investment or business income. This technique is referred to with different names but ultimately leads many people to retire much earlier than traditionally thought.

The goal is to purchase or create assets that will pay for your monthly expenses and have some remaining for investment. An example of these could be a side business that starts from a hobby and blooms into a fully functioning stream of income. Another example is to purchase a business that is currently mismanaged but you could buy it for a fair price and increase the value over time.

What skills do you have that could add value to the community? Whatever you are interested in, there can be a demand for it, if you market it properly. There are tons of ideas out there with low startup costs, especially in the service industry. "The $100 Startup" by Chris Guillebeau is a good read to get your mind thinking of different ideas. "Mind Your Business" by Ilana Griffo may be a good book to get you started on making progress with a specific idea. It doesn't matter what you choose as long as you commit to something and do it to the best of your ability. Figure out how to add value and you will be rewarded in proportion to that.

I chose apartment investing and property management because they are stable businesses that have recurring payments each month. There was also little cost initially because I started by renting a room in my first house, then moved into a duplex, and continued upgrading from there. Property management was one of those that I naturally had to become pretty good at if I wanted my investments to perform. I also have a big network of contacts that help me manage the properties and I enjoy coordinating logistics and forecasting with other investors.

I like to recommend people get involved in businesses where they can offer subscripted goods or services that yield recurring income. I also prefer investments that pay dividends or recurring interest. Regardless of which strategies you use, the goal is to create systems that add value to the community and generate a recurring income to replace your earned income.

Notice that I said to build a system of businesses and/or investments that generate recurring monthly income. I did not say create a new job for yourself and it is important to know the difference between managing a business and owning a job. If you manage a business you have key people and systems in place that can deal with the day-to-day operations and provide value to your customers. Think of a machine that has all the parts to yield the result that you want.

What if you could have a vacation rental at the beach or the mountains that generates $24,000 a year from Airbnb while giving you a month in the fall to enjoy it with your family? How about a 4-unit apartment building that sends you $3,600 a month in income? The interesting thing about these real estate scenarios is that you could have both of these for a relatively small down payment and replace your earned income within 15 years or less. Investment real estate usually only requires 20% down and we will discuss rentals in the Investments section.

Even if you don't fully commit to this concept and keep a traditional retirement account, you can't help but see the value of additional income. Most people are simply not dedicated enough to save up for retirement. Building a part-time business or partnership along with having a rental property may be a good idea even if it supplements your retirement.

Another beautiful thing about creating streams of income from investments or businesses is that you aren't confined to retirement at a set age. It gives you control and flexibility to make the best choices for you and your family. You don't have to worry about complicated investment strategies or getting penalized if you withdraw early.

You are never worried that you will get laid off from your job because you have built and manage a machine that pays for all of your expenses. "Rich Dad Poor Dad" by Robert Kiyosaki was one of the first books I ever read on this alternate retirement concept and explains the process well. It was an eye-opening experience that led me to study personal finance heavily, over the past 10 years.

CHAPTER 9
INVESTMENTS

This is a disclaimer stating that I am not a certified financial planner and that I do not give financial advice. I may state what I invest in but this is not an endorsement of any product and I always recommend becoming familiar with any investment before diving in.

With any investment, there is a certain amount of risk involved and the reward should always outweigh the risk. Please research all products thoroughly and discuss them with your team of authorized advisors, accountants, and attorneys.

There are many investment vehicles today and it can easily become overwhelming and confusing. I am going to go over the basics and try to simplify ideas that may yield a return on your money. The important factor to remember is that an asset produces income or a capital gain, while a liability takes capital from you. I encourage people to first learn about investments, specifically ones they find interesting and become knowledgeable about while continuing to learn as they actively invest and grow.

Cash, Precious Metals, & Commodities

Physical cash does not produce a return unless you purchase or create an asset that generates income, interest/dividend payments, or buy something that you sell later for a capital gain. This is important to understand because if you are saving cash with no return, it is losing value through inflation. To my knowledge, the only time holding cash would be beneficial is if the economy were deflationary and not inflationary. This has not happened since the 1930s and is when the prices of goods and services are decreasing due to the contraction of the currency supply.

One option is to put your cash into a Certificate of Deposit (CD) Account, Money Market Account (MMA), or traditional savings account that will earn some interest for you while being protected with the same deposit insurance (FDIC) that covers your checking account. The interest yields on these accounts tend to be very low today, less than 1% APY but was a common option in the past. If you put cash into a CD it is parked there for the term of the CD, as opposed to the Money Market and savings accounts, which are a little more flexible. Be sure to understand if you will have access to the funds or the time required for maturity.

Currency is a very important part of our financial system and we need to save some for reserves and actively invest a majority if we expect to become financially independent. It is also possible to borrow currency at low-interest rates to maximize returns while investing. As long as you are making a higher return on your investment than the cost of interest, you can keep the difference for yourself. Maybe you have heard the term Other People's Money (OPM) which talks about leveraging capital from others to create a profit.

As we stated in the savings chapter, I like to keep six months of reserves on hand for personal and business expenses. We have seen more businesses close during crisis mainly because they did not have reserves on hand, were overleveraged with debt, and their income shrank drastically.

I highly recommend saving cash reserves before you start any investing. It is important to have a buffer of cash because things will go wrong at times and you will need funds to fall back on. Cash reserves can be valuable and I try to use credit as much as possible when investing if I can get favorable terms and low-interest rates.

Precious metals have served as money for thousands of years and I save 10% of my wealth in physical gold and silver. I do not intend to sell or trade these until they become overvalued and I can exchange them for items such as real estate or a business that is equally valuable and produces income at that time.

I like to track the gold/silver ratio which shows how many ounces of silver it takes to purchase one ounce of gold. This can be an indicator when one metal is overpriced compared to the other and a good time to exchange. There are other metrics such as the DJIA measured in gold and pricing everyday items in gold or silver, which shows the purchasing power of the metals increasing or decreasing over time. The book "Guide to Investing in Gold and

Silver" by Mike Maloney and his "Hidden Secrets of Money" series on YouTube are great baseline resources for learning about precious metals.

The spot price is the market price that people are willing to buy or sell at. Generally, you will pay a premium over spot, depending on the demand for metals and the availability of the product. For silver, it tends to be around $1 per ounce in premium and around $50 an ounce on gold in low to normal demand times. These are generalizations and can vary depending on what specific products you are buying and the demand at the time. The US coins tend to have higher premiums than other bullion products in the market.

I mostly use sites such as **www.golddealer.com, www.goldsilver.com,** or **www.apmex.com** to source or sell holdings. These are a few that I have found to be reputable over time and charge a fair premium over the spot price. You can also do a Google search for local coin and precious metal dealers near you to conduct business face to face. Be sure to look up reviews on companies through Google and the Better Business Bureau, as there are companies that sell counterfeit metals or overpriced numismatic coins.

Gold and silver are a more stable account of value when compared to fiat currencies that lose value through inflation over time. Our dollar has lost around 95% of its purchasing power since 1913, thus increasing the dollar price of gold from $20.67 to over $1800 per ounce in the same period. I view these metals as money and a store of value but you will hear most people refer to them as commodities.

Physical precious metals have no counterparty risk because we do not rely on anyone else to regulate the price and there is no debt attached to them. An ounce of gold in your hands is simply that and will remain that forever until you transfer ownership. The only downside I see to physical metals is storage and keeping it safe but I believe the reward outweighs the risk, especially if you have a home safe or pay for monthly vault storage.

Commodities are the raw materials and building blocks of our society. They can mainly be divided into 4 different categories that are: Metals, Energy, Livestock & Meat, and Agricultural. Futures contracts are a way you can purchase or sell a specified amount of a commodity at a future date. Airlines and farms are examples of companies that may purchase futures contracts of oil so that they can budget for the upcoming year and control expenses that come along with operating the business.

You can also speculate in these futures contracts if you believe a commodity will trade higher or lower over the respective time. With the speculation concept, most would sell the contract before taking a delivery or having to come up with the product to sell, while hopefully increasing their account balance by the rise or fall in price. These strategies can be very technical and should be viewed as highly risky because of the leverage that is used and the possibility of volatility. These futures contracts are what directly affect the market price of commodities through supply and demand. The lower the supply, the higher the prices, provided there is a demand for the item.

These items can also be traded through different ETFs. A commodity ETF will trade on the underlying price of the commodity. A commodity producer's ETF is a fund that holds stock of companies that produce the commodities. You can find various ETFs that hold energy, agricultural, or other commodity-producing companies.

While you can trade paper commodities and derivatives, the reason I placed them with cash and metals is that you can also purchase the physical form of commodities through various companies and the futures contracts that we talked about earlier. Just like precious metals, I like the concept of owning the physical and primary wealth of items with inherent value.

The challenge with owning physical commodities such as oil, corn, metals, or cattle is the storage aspect and finding a buyer. That is why most people purchase the paper option of commodities and trade them with ETFs. Of course, just like any other paper asset, the problem is that you don't physically own the product and the paper you hold is a representation of the item.

One interesting way to be affiliated with commodities is to store or transport them. This is more of a business idea that deals with commodities, but something that could yield a profit. Overall, whether you are purchasing and selling physical commodities or trading in paper contracts, there can be profit made if you take time to learn and become proficient.

Stocks, Mutual Funds, ETFs, REITs, Bonds, Lending, Cryptocurrencies, & FOREX

What do these investments have in common? They are all "paper" or digital assets and some of the most common securities, debts, and currencies. You can trade most of these through accounts on your computer or hire companies to manage them. Today, many brokerage accounts offer free trading if you make the trades yourself and only charge a fee if you use a manager. Be sure to keep an eye on these fees and expenses as they can cut into your profits.

There are several different **trading strategies** with the most common being day trading (1-day max, no overnight holds), swing trading (several days, sometimes weeks), or position trading (longer approach up to years). If you are interested in trading any investment, you will need to decide which specific strategy to use.

Stocks are ownership or equity shares of a corporation. Most stocks you will see are publicly-traded companies on a stock exchange such as the New York Stock Exchange or NASDAQ. Each publicly-traded company has a ticker symbol that is traded on a specific stock exchange of that geographic region. An example is the ticker symbol "AAPL" which represents Apple that makes the iPhone and is traded on the NASDAQ exchange in the U.S. You can search on various trading platforms for any company or ETF ticker symbol and their respective exchanges.

All publicly-traded companies share financials quarterly so you can track trends and values over time. There are many financials to look at when buying stocks and some include the Price to Earnings Ratio (P/E Ratio), Dividend Yield, Earnings per Share, and Return on Equity. Familiarize yourself with these terms and what they mean to you as an investor. It is very important to explore these financials, especially when picking individual stocks.

A few apps you can use to purchase stocks from your smartphone are Charles Schwab, Webull, Robinhood, and E*TRADE. The normal hours for stock trading are Monday through Friday from 9:30 AM to 4:00 PM EST, but can also be traded after hours with the proper accounts.

In addition to individual company stocks, there are indexes (also called indices), that track a group of stocks such as the Dow Jones Industrial Average (DJIA), Standard & Poor's 500 (S&P 500), or NASDAQ Composite. These indexes are measurement indicators of portions of the market. The DJIA is a price-weighted index that tracks 30 large, publicly-traded companies on the New York Stock Exchange and NASDAQ Exchange. The S&P 500 is a market-capitalization-weighted index of the 500 largest U.S. publicly traded companies.

There are Mutual Funds and Exchange Traded Funds that closely resemble these indexes. The ETFs and Mutual funds based on these indexes are designed to mitigate more of the risk when compared to picking individual stocks. Warren Buffet and many professional investors recommend the average person to invest in a product that follows the S&P 500 or total market index, with low fees for the long term.

Mutual Funds are professionally managed funds that pool currency from many investors to purchase securities. The currency that you have input purchases a share of the mutual fund and an interest in the profits and losses of that fund.

Many mutual funds will be based on an index such as the S&P500, DJIA, MSCI Emerging Markets, or others. "VTSAX" is an example of a Vanguard total stock market indexed mutual fund while "VTBLX" is their indexed bond mutual fund. Many other companies offer indexed mutual funds and the important thing is to choose one with a proven track record, low fees, and an amount that you can afford.

There are also actively managed mutual funds where a fund manager or team chooses the investments in an attempt to outperform the indexed market. Imagine putting your cash into a container with other people and then shaking that container up. A fund manager will then take those funds and purchase assets that they think will grow over time.

They may invest in equities (stocks), fixed income (bonds), and money markets (similar to cash), depending on your risk tolerance. Some funds may invest in several categories and other more complex instruments called derivatives. It's important to understand what your funds are purchasing.

Be sure to look at all the costs associated with mutual funds, especially actively managed funds. Explore sites such as **www.nerdwallet.com** or **www.fool.com** to get a better understanding of investing and see how they rank the different companies that offer mutual funds and other investments.

"Common Sense on Mutual Funds" by John Bogle may be a good read to learn about mutual funds before you make your first investment. You can purchase mutual funds through a brokerage account with companies such as Vanguard, Charles Schwab, TD Ameritrade, Merrill Lynch, Fidelity, and many more.

Exchange-Traded Funds (ETFs) are investment funds traded on stock exchanges that hold assets such as stocks, commodities, currencies, or bonds. It is similar to a mutual fund in the respect that it purchases investments but differs in that it can be traded many times a day, whereas a mutual fund can only be traded once a day. There is also no minimum investment like many mutual funds, which makes it accessible for more people.

ETFs have a ticker symbol similar to a stock because they are traded on the same exchanges. Do your research on the different Index ETFs such as VTI, SPY, and VOO, as this can be a good way to hold a diversified position in the equity markets. There are also bond ETFs such as BND or AGG, that are supposed to be less risky but generally produce a lower return. You can purchase ETFs through the same accounts that you purchase stocks. Be sure to watch out for the expense ratio like with mutual funds.

I prefer index ETFs such as Vanguard's "VTI" or "VOO" over mutual funds because the fees are low, there is no minimum investment, the returns are great over time, and I can self-manage on my smartphone.

Real Estate Investment Trusts (REITs) are real estate investment companies that purchase and/or manage various categories of real estate. You purchase shares of stock in these companies just like you would any other company. There are commercial companies that focus on retail space for malls, offices, storage, and more; whereas residential companies focus on single-family homes, condos, or apartments to rent for housing people.

REITs are a way for you to own stock in companies that own and/or manage real estate without the day-to-day management of tenants or repairs. Ticker symbol "O" is one REIT that I like and has proven to be a stable company with growing dividends for over 26 years. It is also one of the few companies that pay dividends monthly, instead of quarterly.

There are also REIT ETFs if you want to have a more diversified approach. "REZ", "XLRE, and "VNQ" are examples of REIT ETFs that hold a basket of Real Estate Investment Trusts in the market. Just as with normal stocks, these ETFs should reduce some of the risks when compared to picking individual companies.

Like any other stock or ETF, you can purchase these through smartphone apps such as Charles Schwab, Webull, Robinhood, E*TRADE, and more.

Bonds are IOUs from a specific corporation or government. When you buy a bond, you're lending money to the organization that issued it. The bondholder receives interest and is usually paid out once or twice per year. The bondholder will also receive the initial principal at a specified future date, called maturity.

The 3 main types of bonds are US Treasury bonds which fund the Federal government, Municipal bonds that finance local government, and corporate bonds which raise capital for corporations.

The most common way to gain income from bonds is to receive interest payments over time and the principal at maturity. For example, a US Treasury bond may make interest payments twice a year for 10 years and then pay the principal back at the 10-year mark. The interest rate will be determined by the market when you purchase the bond.

If interest rates rise while you are holding the bond, the value of the bond will drop because any new bonds issued will be paying a higher interest rate. If interest rates go down while you are holding a bond, your bond is more valuable because you are earning higher than current market interest on that bond. You may sell these bonds before maturity but interest rates will determine if you can sell at a discount or a premium.

Generally, bonds are considered a safe investment and can be secured by collateral or unsecured. Bonds are rated by their risk of the company or government issuing them, so be sure to check out the credit rating and financials of the organization, along with their track record of repayments over time.

Credit ratings range from AAA, which is best, to D being the worst. Anything BB or lower is known as junk bonds or high yield. As the credit rating is reduced, the interest should be higher since you are taking on a higher risk. You can check out credit ratings by the big 3 raters at Standard and Poor's, Fitch, and Moody's.

There are many places to purchase bonds and most people use an online brokerage to do so. **www.worthybonds.com** is an online resource where you can purchase bonds that support small businesses in the US. You can use **www.treasurydirect.gov** or visit your local bank if you want to buy US Treasury bonds, and many online brokerages such as Ally Invest, Fidelity, or Vanguard to purchase various bonds.

There are several ways that you can lend currency to earn interest. One popular method is **Peer to Peer (P2P) lending** and when you act as the lender to an individual or business, through an online service. Although similar to purchasing bonds, there are a few key differences.

The main difference is that you are lending directly to small businesses or individuals instead of governments or larger corporations. Also, with P2P loans, you receive principal and interest payments monthly instead of biannual interest payments from a bond with principal at maturity.

Perhaps, you are lending to an individual who is consolidating debt or maybe a business that needs capital for growth. There will be online resources that connect the two of you, such as Prosper or Street Shares. These are just two examples in a realm of possibilities where you lend money to entities for an established interest rate. **www.moneyunder30.com** is a good place to start when searching for reputable P2P lending sites.

You could also purchase existing notes or create loans to gain monthly income and interest. Before doing this, it is wise to speak with an attorney who is well versed in contract law as well as investigate the entity's credit and ability to repay. There is a book called "Note Investing Made Easier" by Martin Saenz that may be helpful to learn about real estate note investing and "The Insider's Guide to Private Lending" by Jeff Levin that could help you structure the details of your first loan.

Cryptocurrencies are relatively new when compared to most other investments and were introduced in 2009 with the most popular cryptocurrency, Bitcoin. Since then, there have been thousands of alt currencies created in the market. One great thing about the crypto markets is that they are open 24 hours a day and 7 days a week, so there is no delay in trading and they are highly liquid.

You can visit exchanges such as Coinbase, Binance, Webull, and more to purchase various cryptocurrencies. Even if you only have small amounts to invest with it is easy to purchase a fraction of the cryptocurrency with US Dollars or other currencies. You can securely store cryptocurrencies for long-term holding in a digital wallet offered by such companies as Coinbase, Exodus, or others.

Some people are trading various cryptocurrencies as the market fluctuates to make a profit and others mine cryptos for profit. Mining is when you have computers and graphic processing units dedicated to solving the math that is required to complete a cryptocurrency transaction. In return, the miners are rewarded with an amount of the respective cryptocurrency.

There are several blockchain ETFs, such as "BLOK" and "LEGR" which invest in the blockchain technology that cryptocurrencies and other digital systems operate within. "GBTC" is an investment vehicle that gives investors exposure to Bitcoin without having to securely hold it. I am sure there are various other funds, ETFs, and derivatives of cryptocurrency that will transpire.

I'm spending more time learning about cryptocurrency and have some speculating on Bitcoin. I appreciate the technology that goes into these and also it being outside of central bank control. If you want to learn more about cryptocurrencies there are a ton of YouTube videos on the subject, while the books "The Basics of Bitcoins and Blockchains" by Antony Lewis and "The Crypto Trader" by Glen Goodman may be of benefit.

FOREX traders look to make a profit by betting that a currency's value will either appreciate or depreciate against another currency.

For example, the price between the EUR/USD fluctuates over time and can be profitable if you buy or sell with the right timing and deviation in value. There are many different currencies within the FOREX markets that you can trade. These markets are open 24 hours a day, 5.5 days a week because of the differences in time zones and exchanges. Check out **babypips.com/learn** for more information on trading currencies.

A friend who trades currency recommended a book called "Trading for a Living" by Dr. Alexander Elder and said there are tons of YouTube videos that can show you the basics. He also stated that he uses FX Choice for a broker and a program call MT4 to assist with trading strategies.

I know very little about currency trading for profit but I understand the basic idea of exchange rates and fees. I have learned this from traveling all over the world and becoming aware of the fees and exchange rates that eat into your funds.

Annuities

Annuities are agreements between you and an insurance company where you input cash as payments or a lump sum, in exchange for a payout of guaranteed recurring income during retirement.

These can be good for people who have stored a large amount of cash or who have additional income while working and want a stable stream of income through retirement. Be sure to watch out for surrender fees, administrative & management fees, and commissions.

The two main types of annuities are Immediate or Deferred Income. As the name hints, an immediate annuity is when you input a lump sum of cash to gain an immediate revenue stream for the rest of your life, while a deferred income annuity is one in which you pay monthly for a future revenue stream.

Within these two types, you may be able to choose a fixed, variable, or indexed rate of return. A fixed return will provide a fixed interest rate return and a fixed payout amount. A variable product may invest in different investments that are not guaranteed but could yield a higher return and the payout may fluctuate with the markets. An indexed annuity may have fixed and variable features. In these indexed policies, interest credits are linked to an external index such as the S&P 500 but contain a minimum guaranteed interest.

Annuities may be sold by many financial companies but only insurance companies can issue an annuity. Most annuities are regulated by the state in which the policy is issued, just like other forms of insurance. Visit **https://content.naic.org/** for more information on the National Association of Insurance Commissioners or go directly to your state Office of Insurance Regulation to find out more about the insurance companies doing business in your state.

On the contrary to fixed annuities, a variable annuity is regulated by the SEC because of the securities it purchases. Be sure to do your research on the specific company and the track record of that company in the past while completing due diligence through the regulating agencies.

Five firms review insurance companies by considering their financials, ability to pay, amount of cash on hand, and other measures that are important to view in addition to the regulating authorities. They are A.M. Best, Fitch, KBRA, Moody's, and Standard & Poor's. Take a look at their rating with these companies, your state regulating authorities, and even online searching can give you good information based on customer experiences.

You may choose to purchase an annuity through many brokers such as Raymond James or Merrill Lynch. You could also go directly to insurance companies such as American Equity Investment Life Holding Company, MetLife, New York Life, Prudential, or many more.

Life Insurance Policies

There are several different types of life insurance but we will discuss the main three types. They are **term life, whole life, and universal life**. The essential question you need to ask is "Do I want coverage for a specific term or do I want to purchase coverage for my whole life?" From there you can dive deeper as to what additional benefits the policies have.

The first and most simple policy is the term life insurance policy. This is not usually considered an investment but protection against the inevitable. Just as the name states, you will be paying a premium for life insurance during the term of the policy. If you die within that allotted period, the policy will pay the death benefit to the designated party, called the beneficiary. If you do not die within that term, the premiums paid are forfeited.

Some advisors may recommend 10x your annual salary for the amount of insurance needed. However, it is your choice and depends on how much debt you have, the equity you have in investments, children in college, and how much you want to leave behind. I have a term policy that would extinguish any consumer debt, pay for burial expenses, and leave a little leftover. My investments would transfer to my family and there is sufficient equity and income to take care of them.

Most employers will generally offer a term policy for their employees, while a whole or universal life policy is oftentimes purchased by the individual. In addition to an employer-based term policy, there are also several other sources where you can purchase a term policy. **www.bestow.com** is an online resource where you can get a free quote for term life insurance or you can call or visit insurance companies directly such as John Hancock, State Farm, New York Life, and many more.

The next two policies are **whole life** and **universal life** policies. There are many variants of these policies and can differ greatly, so it is important to research the insurance companies. These policies offer permanent life insurance options for the duration of your years and can operate similarly to a savings account with a cash value feature.

Whole life and universal life insurance policies can act similar to annuities in the concept that you input cash as payments or a lump sum to purchase premiums that will eventually payout in the future. The main difference is that annuities pay out income, usually monthly during retirement, while life insurance is a one-time death benefit. However, some policies may also accumulate a cash value like a savings account.

In addition to the death benefit, you may be able to take a loan on the cash value accumulated within the policy, which the death benefit would pay off when that arrives. For example, if you pay into a policy at $200 per month for 20 years, your cash value may be $48,000 plus any gains depending on which funds the insurance company invested in. You could be able to take that out as a loan and pay it back with minimal interest while you are alive. The idea is when you die, the death benefit should be large enough to pay off the loan, extinguish any other debts while leaving money left over for burial and other costs to the beneficiary.

Two resources that explain these concepts more completely are the books "Money, Wealth, Life Insurance" by Jake Thompson and "Becoming your Own Banker" by R. Nelson Nash.

As stated with annuities, five firms review insurance companies by considering their financials, ability to pay, amount of cash on hand, and other measures that are important to view in addition to the regulating authorities. They are A.M. Best, Fitch, KBRA, Moody's, and Standard & Poors. Take a look at their rating with these companies, your state regulating authorities, and even online searching can give you good information based on customer experiences.

This is a simplified scenario and I recommend speaking with a professional insurance broker who can shop multiple companies and give you advice that meets your long-term goals. I believe everyone should look into some form of life insurance or leave capital so we do not burden our families with the inevitable.

Income-Producing or Capital Gains Real Estate

Income-producing real estate is one investment I purchase to fund my life's work. The concept here is to create a positive net income after paying all expenses of the property, including the mortgage, repairs, management, and more. I have had years of education and experience doing this and strongly advise gaining a good understanding before you take the plunge into this field. As I have said earlier, make sure you have cash reserves on hand before you decide to invest, especially in real estate that is not liquid and can take many months to sell.

The rent is the most common income stream from a property but can also consist of laundry machines, vending, storage, etc. There are residential rental units, commercial units that you can lease to businesses, storage units for personal belongings or vehicles, warehouses, and many more. I choose residential real estate because there will always be a demand for housing, whereas commercial space can be questionable at times, especially with ever-growing e-commerce businesses.

If you finance a property with a typical 20% down payment, you will have a monthly payment of principal/interest, taxes, and insurance that you will have to pay. You will also have monthly expenses such as repairs, vacancy, management, cleaning, and more that you will have to account for. In general, these expenses average 50% of the income you will take in. The goal is to have a positive net income (also called cash flow) after all these expenses have been paid so you create a stable income stream each month.

As a rule of thumb, the monthly rent should equal at least 1% of the asking price before it is worth analyzing further. This number is a possible indication that there will be enough to leave you with income after all expenses. This is a generality and you need to look at all the expenses and the income produced to arrive at the exact number.

There are many different free spreadsheets online where you can analyze a property to see if it is a good deal for your portfolio. An example is **www.calculator.net/rental-property** or going to **https://kellerink.com/pages/resources** and downloading the Hold Worksheet, which I what I use to analyze each deal.

Another favorite resource is **www.biggerpockets.com** to learn the basics and **www.richdad.com/resources/tools** for calculators and information regarding real estate. Numbers do not lie and it's important to account for income and subtract all expenses to arrive at the amount that you will receive monthly.

You can repeat the process to gain a desired monthly income to fund your life's work. This can replace your income from your job and lead you to financial freedom. Of course, it could lead you to pay out of pocket each month, if you don't calculate your numbers right, so take your time. You do not want to end up with a bad property and tenants that cost you out of pocket each month.

This can be a slow process over time as you save for down payments and increase equity in properties but is one of the most stable and productive investments I have found. I love the concept of recurring income that will survive for a very long time and I can pay a professional manager to collect for me. It may also increase in value over time which increases my net worth in the process. There is something nice about being able to pull in the driveway and look at your investment compared to just owning digital assets.

In addition to a stable stream of income that is derived from a tangible asset, you can leverage the banks' or investors' money to make up most of the capital needed to purchase the rental property. If you wanted to test the waters and get started in a property where you will live in one of the units of a multiple-unit building, you may need to only put down 3%. If the property is strictly for investment as a rental, you will need to put down around 20% of the purchase price, but can still finance the remaining balance.

There are many perks to rental real estate and most of this income can be received by you throughout the year, with little income to pay tax on at the end of the year. You will collect rents monthly and then spend some capital on maintenance, management, and more while being able to deduct all of this and another deduction called depreciation. The IRS allows you to depreciate the residential rental property over 27.5 years because that is their assessment of a useful life span.

What this means is you can deduct the depreciation and all property expenses from the income received and only pay tax on the amount that remains. It is a powerful way to increase your monthly income with minimal taxable gain. Hire a competent CPA and discuss this concept thoroughly to gain a better understanding of the tax laws pertaining to rental real estate.

Of course, because rentals are tangible there is a lot more responsibility and you are dealing with people that have needs and wants. It is not an investment for people who aren't willing to respond to repair requests and solve problems as they arise.

As with any investment, there is a certain amount of risk that you take on at purchase and management. Real estate can be a massive headache if you don't have the right team in place that will help you through the roller coaster of owning property. You will have problems with tenants and repairs over time and will need a competent property manager and vendor contacts when these issues arise. You will also need a competent accountant and attorney for your annual tax returns and if litigation arises from liability on the properties. Also, keeping good insurance and proper entity structures is a necessity to protect your investment and yourself.

If you are interested in rental real estate, I recommend reading the book "Hold" by Steve Chader and "The Book on Rental Property Investing" by Brandon Turner. A great podcast is the Real Estate Guys Radio Show or The Real Estate Strategies Podcast with Ken McElroy. You can find various other resources at the back of this book in the Recommendations section.

Capital gains real estate investments work very differently and you have to be a little more involved throughout the process. When you stop buying, renovating, and reselling real estate, the income stops just like a job if you do not go to work. I have done this several times to gain funds to reinvest in rentals or other income-producing opportunities.

The process is to buy at a price that allows you to wholesale to another individual who will renovate the building and resell it, or renovate it yourself and sell it for a profit. A rule of thumb is to purchase the property at 70% of the After Repair Value, minus any repairs. This should leave enough profit margin for upgrades, carrying costs, and time spent.

You will need a good real estate agent that can look up comparable sales and let you know what the property could be worth after renovation, so you will know how much to put into the property. You will also need this agent to market the property and sell it quickly so you can recover your costs and profits. One of the most important things to remember is to not over or under improve a property. Look at the comparable homes in the area and renovate them to a similar quality. If you over renovate you could spend way more money on the property that you will not get back when you sell.

There are also carrying costs that you need to be aware of while you own a property and are in the renovation process. These can include property taxes, insurance, landscaping, and any interest or points associated if you financed the property. Be sure to include these in your budget.

It is important to become familiar with pricing on renovation materials and various contractors that will help you through the process. Be careful with your budgeting on renovations and also the cost to sell the property with real estate commissions and closing costs. Renovation costs can range drastically depending on the finishes you choose and the contractors doing the work. The average cost to sell a property is roughly 8%, with 6% going to the real estate agents and an extra percent or more for closing costs.

Capital gains taxes are another big factor to consider when doing this, especially if you are flipping a property inside of one year. As we stated in the taxes section, short-term capital gains can take an immediate 15% to 20% of the proceeds on the sale, so be sure to consider this when you are analyzing the deal.

You can make a lot of money doing this but you need to be aware of the local economy and what part of the real estate cycle we are in. A lot of people got caught holding real estate in 2008 that was overvalued when prices dropped, along with having too much debt on the property. Of course, this made it very difficult to sell or refinance and escalated the foreclosures.

The book "Flip" by Rick Villani and "The Book on Estimating Rehab Costs" by Brandon Turner are great resources if you are interested in flipping real estate for capital gains. Check the Recommendations section in the back for more books and information.

Creating or Improving Businesses

There are many different ways that you can add value to the local community. One of the most efficient ways is to provide goods and services through business ventures. You could dive into a full-time business or work on a part-time project that you are interested in. Regardless of which route you choose, be smart with having proper reserves and be willing to dedicate the required time to ensure success. Many people severely underestimate the time and capital that it takes to create and sustain a successful business.

"Side Hustle: From Idea to Income in 27 Days" by Chris Guillebeau may be helpful when thinking of potential ideas that you can create in the time outside of a full-time job. I chose to start a few side hustles over the years to shift stable employment income to business and investments. I enjoy my day job but realize I'm never going to get wealthy by strictly trading time for dollars. I also understand that banks want to see stable income and reasonable reserves for purchasing investment real estate.

The key with part-time businesses is to have team members in place to manage it effectively or create systems that take care of your customers. Think back to the passive income concepts.

Outside of the full-time or part-time decision, the next choice is will you create a business from scratch or purchase an existing business. If you are considering purchasing an existing business, the books "Here's the Deal" by Joel Ankney or "HBR Guide to Buying a Small Business" by Richard S. Ruback and Royce Yudkoff may be helpful to navigate contracts and details with the seller. If you are looking to create a new business "The Young Entrepreneur's Guide to Starting and Running a Business" by Steve Mariotti might be a good resource.

Once you decide on full or part-time, creating or purchasing a business, and the type of business, you should do some basic market research to determine if there is a need. Existing businesses in your local area may be helpful to view the actual market and financial data. Talk to people and see if they will sign up for your service or purchase products.

One important thing I have learned is that you need to allocate appropriate time and capital for marketing the idea, especially with startups. "The 1-Page Marketing Plan" by Allan Dib is a great book that can help with getting your product or service in front of potential customers.

Another important thing to understand is that you have to bring in revenue, regardless of how much fun you are having. I know this is common sense but sometimes we get off course. I challenge people to offer subscriptive goods or services because of the recurring income and stability that comes with that. For example, one company may sell socks that have sporadic sales throughout the year, while another company provides a membership that sends new socks to customers twice a year. This is just one idea but you get the point of recurring income compared to random sales throughout the weeks.

Regardless of your model, business is a numbers game and we must know what it takes to be profitable. Without profit, you cannot grow and serve customers, nor your employees. For example, to bring in a million dollars of revenue annually from managing real estate, I need approximately 840 accounts that yield $100 per month. From there, I deduct operating expenses, taxes, etc. to arrive at the profit. It is very similar to doing the math on the personal income statement. Then, reinvest that profit into more assets that generate income or gains.

The goal should be to provide maximum value to the greatest number of customers and you will be rewarded in proportion to that. I believe that is why technology businesses are making a fortune today because they have streamlined processes and serve a tremendous amount of people.

CHAPTER 10
ASSET ALLOCATION

With all of these choices, where do you start? I can tell you from experience, investing can be overwhelming, especially if you try to do a little of everything. When I first started investing in real estate, I was trying way too many different strategies. It became tiresome and burned me out until I decided to focus on a more specific approach. My criteria for purchasing are also very clear now and lets me know quickly if it is a good deal.

Through trial and error and a lot of education over the years, I am now knowledgeable about buying and managing property, while clear on my financial goals. I know what a bad investment is because I have bought a few but have learned to focus on the numbers and create income after all expenses are paid.

I can attribute a lot of getting clear on goals to Gary Keller and his book "The ONE Thing". He challenges you to choose the one thing today that would contribute to the most benefit in the future and accomplish it. Tim Ferriss wrote "The 4 Hour Workweek" which is similar in concept by doing less while gaining better results. These are about getting clear and becoming more efficient with your time, which is your most valuable resource.

I propose finding a subject that interests you and become knowledgeable in it before you branch out into several asset classes. A lot of financial planners will set you up to diversify your portfolio in only paper assets, but as Warren Buffet would say "Wide diversification is only required when investors do not understand what they are doing." We will never be great at everything and need to understand that with investing.

Everyone has an opinion and a lot of times free information can cost you a lot of money. In my experience, it takes time to learn about specific subjects while actively investing in a plan that you feel is right for your life. The idea is to focus on creating income and capital gains while learning from mistakes and becoming more efficient over time.

In the 627-page book named "Money" by Tony Robbins, he interviews many of the world's top investors, money managers, and financial minds. I found it to be a decent book with some value but I will spare you the time and we will skip to page 391; he interviews Ray Dalio, one of the world's top hedge fund managers and gets his input on investing and asset allocation. This is the main reason I purchased the book and his advice is as follows:

He recommends 30% in stocks, for example, an ETF based on the S&P 500 Index for diversification within the stock market, 15% in 7 to 10-year Treasuries, 40% in 20 to 25-year Treasuries, 7.5% in

gold, and 7.5% in commodities, while having a fiduciary handle it for you. Of course, this is not his exact recipe in what he does for his clients, it's a general overview of what he recommends for the average investor.

Another strategy and easy-to-read example is "The Simple Path to Wealth" by JL Collins. It shares a similar but less diversified approach that is very easy to follow. This is advice that Warren Buffet similarly recommends to the average person who doesn't want to learn a lot about investing, yet not lose out to inflation.

The idea is to purchase equities in an indexed mutual fund or ETF, such as "VTSAX" Mutual Fund or "VTI" Exchange Traded Fund. As we have discussed in the investments chapter, you can purchase this mutual fund and other indexed funds by going to a broker such as Vanguard, Fidelity, TD Ameritrade, etc. You can purchase the indexed ETFs directly through an app like Robinhood, Webull, E*TRADE, etc. that has access to the stock exchange on your phone.

These ETFs or Mutual Funds own a portion of all the stocks in the market, which gives you broad diversification and a lower downside when compared to picking individual stocks. You can purchase the total market ETFs that have exposure to around 3000 companies; or you can purchase an ETF such as "VOO" which holds America's large-cap 500 companies, also known as the S&P 500. Both share similar returns over time while minimizing risk. While you are younger you will put most of your investment funds into this (Approximately 80%).

As you get closer to retirement, start taking a higher percentage that you feel comfortable with and shift it into "VBTLX" Mutual Fund or the "BND" ETF. These are bond indexes that produce a lower yield but generally less volatility. The key is starting early and contributing regularly to maximize growth, over time.

I'm sure you will see similar responses in investments with a variance of percentages if you talk to many financial planners today. While these may work fine for most people, there are always more ways that can yield the ultimate result, which is financial freedom and the ability to retire. The key is taking it head-on, calculating the numbers, and coming up with a solution that works for you.

My perspective is a little different but I think it can be helpful for people who want to grab the bull by the horns and be more active in their investing approach. I prefer recurring income and capital gains in asset classes that I am knowledgeable in. I have amounts invested in ETFs and precious metals but my main focus is income-producing business and real estate rentals. I consider the diversification a means to capital gains that I will reinvest into income-producing business and real estate, at a later date.

Learn about value investing and how to create income through rents, dividends, interest, royalties, and capital gains, while minimizing taxes and expenses along the way. There is a big difference between value and price and as you gain experience, you will learn to see the value-add opportunities in the investments you deem appropriate. Don't be so focused on price that you step over a dollar to pick up a quarter. I have learned to be very interested in what the future may look like because technology and culture are changing the way we do business each day.

If you create or expand businesses and investments, you will be rewarded for it in proportion to how well it serves the market. It has to add value to people's lives and must be marketed efficiently. There is usually an immense amount of work that comes before the money and the perceived success, so be sure to dedicate sufficient time to get a business started or growing an existing one.

Building businesses and managing real estate is a lot more to juggle than just putting money in the stock market but it can also be much more rewarding. Today, I am reaping the rewards from positive decisions that I made years ago and have created income that is sustainable and recurring. I challenge you to find something worth working hard on and that you believe in.

Understand that something-for-nothing concepts that sound too good to be true, usually are, and turning your money over to people is a common way to get burned. The key is creating stable income streams that will pay you the amount needed to fund your life's work. Multiple streams of income are my approach to ensure that even in economically challenging situations I will have the means to support my families' lifestyle.

You can talk to many financial planners and many will tell you to place your money in mostly paper assets, under their management. I want you to think outside the box and understand that some of these people are getting rich off of you from commissions and management fees. Not only are you losing through fund expenses but you have also lost control. Educate yourself and be active in your investments and life. It is your retirement and ultimately your responsibility.

If you recall from the income statement section, I said that I only spend around 40% of my income on expenses. I live very comfortably, yet modestly, while still finding time to do most anything that I would want to do in life.

From my 40% of expenses, I set aside 5% for personal education and charity, 5% goes to travel and family experiences, while the remaining 30% goes to normal living expenses such as taxes, housing, insurance, auto, etc. These are a few things I find value in outside of investing and it helps me to achieve balance and recharging after hard work throughout the year.

This allows me to take **60% of my income and invest** in the following ways:

20% invested in business ventures

20% purchases income-producing apartments

10% goes to ROTH IRA and taxable brokerage account

10% purchases physical gold and silver bullion

I analyze this twice a year and rebalance each category, as needed. You can use this asset allocation as loose guidelines for creating your portfolio or completely redesign the numbers to fit your goals.

Take a look at the supplied balance sheet; I have designed it to calculate percentages of your net worth as you type in amounts, so it's easy to stay on track.

The beauty of this portfolio to me is that I have a lot of control over it and I'm not relying on someone to tell me if I can retire. I manage the business and property managers, physically purchase gold and silver, and self-manage investments in the brokerage accounts. I research charities that are productive in the community and try to add value in that capacity. Financial/real estate seminars and books that I find interesting are a part of my educational growth.

The investment in travel, especially with my family, has yielded me a lifetime of memories and perspectives on subjects that I would have never been able to appreciate. I am sure percentages will change as my needs change but this is where I currently am in life and what I have found to be effective.

It pays me monthly income from business and real estate investments, has growth in the total stock market, insurance for downtimes with the metals, and I keep 6 months of reserves to cover all of my personal and business expenses. There is also a term life insurance policy that will pay off any debts and cover funeral expenses when that day arrives.

Many of these investments and expenses pay dividends to my overall health. I believe it to be a conservative and safe portfolio that can weather the storms of uncertainty. It hasn't broken any records but with consistent effort has given me the ability to live life on my terms.

Without starting with the income statement and balance sheet, not much else will be beneficial. It is imperative to start with those numbers as a baseline and compound your income through investments while keeping expenses reasonable. This is the way many wealthy people have gotten where they are today.

Reading "The Millionaire Next Door" by Stanley & Danko opened my eyes to real statistics on high-net-worth individuals and how most of them live compared to the illusory social media lifestyle that we see on the internet. Understand that social media life is that person's best life snapshot and that we all face challenges. Don't be fooled or concerned with keeping up with the Joneses'; focus on your plan and execute until it is realized.

It is not easy, but is simple and only takes dedication to the formula of keeping expenses reasonable and generating enough income to cover them. Create a machine that will finance your freedom. This is true independence from a system that otherwise enslaves us by taking our time from what we love and gives us bits of paper in return. We have unlimited potential and it's time to wake up and realize what we are capable of creating...

CHAPTER 11
INVEST IN YOURSELF

I like to ask people the question: "What would you do with your life if you never had to think about money?" This is the question that I ask myself and it helps me to be more creative. I think about things that I am good at and how I can help those around me with the gifts that I have been given in life. It leads me to create content such as this book to try to help others become better in their lives. Being a part of businesses that provide valuable services and affordable housing is important to me. Veterans' organizations, animal rescue, and healthcare are also topics that I find value in contributing to.

I do not say this to impress you, but simply to give you potential ideas of what skills you possess and how you can make your community a better place. It starts with the change in yourself and then you can create positive changes around you. We are either growing or we are dying; and it is imperative to growth that we figure out our life's work in all areas from health, wealth, and spirituality.

I'm a huge advocate of finding something you find enjoyable because you will create/improve a much better product or service than something you are forced to do just for a paycheck. I encourage investing in yourself through education in whatever subjects you deem to be valuable and finding a way to monetize it. Take your time while learning, network in the business, while saving the reserves and capital required to invest. Don't ever let anyone make you feel rushed into something and ask questions if you do not understand how something works.

Spend time with people who are doing what you want to do. The more time you spend with successful people, the more the ideas, work habits, language, and results will rub off on you. Work with people for free, listen to podcasts, and watch how-to videos on subjects, while remaining open-minded. Find a mentor and team that can help you stay positive in the difficult times that will come and go. Be persistent with your actions each day and think of the most important things you can do that will contribute to the most future success. Get outside of your comfort zone and travel to new areas that can show you alternate ways of doing things.

Take care of your health because we only have one body and we have to live in it for a while. You can amass fortunes, but none of that will matter if you sacrifice your health in the process. Eat healthy, non-processed foods, and view each meal and exercise as overall investment in yourself. If you aren't disciplined enough to do it for yourself, do it for those that you love. Spend time with the ones that are important in your life, especially your children because time doesn't stop for anyone and one day will be filled with regret if you don't.

The hardest step is the first one, but it is the most important in anything we do. If you are working on your health, relationship, finances, spirituality, etc., it takes the idea that you want something different, along with the first step in that direction. Create a game plan to make the changes and track your progress along the way.

At some point, you have to take a chance on yourself. This is what investing in yourself is all about. Taking time to learn about the things that are important to you while putting those ideas to work in real-life application. Build confidence in yourself and remember that knowledge comes from applied information.

According to Earl Nightingale in the Strangest Secret, "Success is the progressive realization of a worthy ideal". It is consistently working toward something you believe in and what I like to call your life's work. He states that for every 25-year-old male that desires success, the average results by the time they get to 65 are as follows: 1 out of 100 will become rich, 4 will become financially independent, 5 will still be working, 54 will be broke. I presume the rest never had a desire to be successful or are dead.

Whatever you deem success to be, if you don't work toward it with daily steps, you are going to be with the rest of the percentages who don't reach their goals. Write it down; that is the first step and then start working toward it. I still keep goals written down on a small piece of paper in my wallet and read it often. It has a deadline on it that reminds me that I won't live forever and holds me accountable.

Even if you fail along the way, the lessons you receive are much better than not starting. You will never win at anything by sitting in the stands and watching those who trained hard and are in the ring.

Run the numbers and track them with the income statement and balance sheet. Figure out ways to expand your means by reducing expenses and increasing your income. Then, create a plan to learn while saving your reserves. Once you have reserves and knowledge, take a step toward a business idea or investment.

Get on **www.fiverr.com** or **www.upwork.com** and enlist the help of people to create an e-commerce site or assist with writing that book you always wanted. You can start small by coming up with a name and a logo, filing the name with the Secretary of State to create an LLC, and opening a business bank account. Go to local meetup groups and network with other entrepreneurs and investors. Start creating a team of vendors and contractors that you want to do business with. There are many small actions that you can do today with the key being to just start. A lot of these steps don't even cost money, so don't let that be an excuse.

There are going to be challenges along the way but the faster you get through these setbacks, the faster you will grow and be able to take on larger obstacles. Learn from every mistake and grow stronger while you continue to progress toward financial freedom. Find a support group or at a minimum a significant other who believes in your ideas and is doing something productive with their lives.

What will you do when you finally achieve financial independence or retire? A lot of people who retire have a difficult time with their life. They never really thought about not working and the routines they have built over the years come to a strange pause. Find something you believe in doing that gives your life purpose.

This book is something that I feel compelled to do because I have a reasonable amount of knowledge on these subjects and most people do not take the time to collect the data and look at available options. My goal with this project is to streamline the road to financial freedom for others.

At the end of the day, it isn't strictly about us, and often the things that make us most satisfied in life are when we contribute to the well-being of the population. You will be surprised at how things that are beneficial to society end up paying you.

Don't allow yourself to be a victim because you choose how to respond in life. Invest in yourself by taking responsibility for healthy physical, financial, mental, and spiritual habits. Invest in your family through quality time and setting them up for success. Invest in your community by contributing something of value; both in time and financial resources. The process is one of balance and the outcome is true freedom.

PART III:
RESOURCES

FINANCIAL GLOSSARY

Account Payable – a liability to a creditor, carried on open account, usually for purchases of goods and services

Account Receivable - a claim against a debtor, carried on open account, usually limited to debts due from the sale of goods and services

Agent – a person or business authorized to act on another's behalf

Amortize - to liquidate or extinguish (a mortgage, debt, or other obligation), especially by periodic payments to the creditor

Annuity - a form of insurance or investment entitling the investor to a series of annual sums

Asset Allocation - The process of dividing investments among different kinds of assets to optimize the risk/reward tradeoff

Asset-Backed Security (ABS) - bonds created from various types of consumer debt

Austrian Economics - Forerunner of unrestrained free-market (libertarian) economics, its central concept is that the coordination of human effort can be achieved only through the combined decisions and judgments of individuals and cannot be forced by an external agency, such as a government

Balance Sheet – a statement of the assets, liabilities, and capital of an entity at a particular point in time

Bankrupt – any insolvent debtor; a person unable to satisfy any just claims made upon him or her

Basis Points – a basis point is a hundredth of a percentage point or 0.01%

Bear Market – A market, especially a stock market, characterized by falling prices

Bonds – an instrument of indebtedness of the bond issuer to the holders

Broker – an agent who buys or sells for a principal on a commission basis without having title to the property

Budget – an estimate of income and expenses for a set period

Bull Market – A market, especially a stock market, characterized by rising prices; the opposite of a bear market

Capital – money or other assets used or available for the production of wealth

Capital Expenditure – money spent by a business or organization on acquiring or maintaining fixed assets, such as land, buildings, and equipment

Capital Gain – a profit from the sale of property or an investment

Capitalization Rate (Cap Rate) – shows the potential rate of return on the investment without financing. **Net Operating Income / Price of the asset**

Cashflow – the total amount of cash being transferred into and out of a business

Cash Flow Statement – a statement that summarizes the amount of cash and cash equivalents entering and leaving a company

Central Bank – an institution that manages the currency and monetary policy of a state or formal monetary union, and oversees commercial banking

Commercial Bank – a bank that offers services to the general public and companies

Commodities – raw materials or primary products that can be bought and sold

Compound Interest – interest computed on the sum of an original principal and accrued interest

Consumer Price Index (CPI) – The Consumer Price Index measures the change in the cost of a representative basket of goods and services such as food, energy, housing, clothing, transportation, medical care, entertainment, and education.

Cost of Goods Sold (COGS) – Costs include all costs of purchase, costs of conversion, and other costs that are incurred in bringing the inventories to their present location and condition. Costs of goods made by the businesses include material, labor, and allocated overhead

Credit – the ability of a customer to obtain goods or services before payment, based on the trust that payment will be made in the future

Cryptocurrency – a digital currency in which encryption technology is used to regulate and generate units of currency and verify the transfer of funds, that works outside of a central bank

Currency – a system of money in general use in a particular country; something that is used as a medium of exchange

Debt – a sum of money that is owed or due. The state of owing money

Debt Coverage Ratio (DCR) – the ratio of operating income available to debt servicing for interest and principal

Debt to Income Ratio (DTI) – the ratio between recurring monthly debt and gross monthly income. It is used to assess the financial credibility and ability of that entity or individual could pay off its debt

Deficit – an excess of expenses over income in a given period

Derivative – having a value deriving from an underlying variable asset

Disposable Income – income that is left after paying taxes and for essential things, such as food and housing

Diversification – to invest in different types of industries, securities, etc.

Dividend – a share in a pro-rata distribution (as of profits) to stockholders

Dollar-Cost Averaging – An investment strategy by which the fund-holder invests fixed sums over time systematically, without regard to the share price at the time

Due Diligence – research and analysis of an organization or investment done in preparation for a business transaction

Earnings Per Share (EPS) – an important financial measure that indicates the profitability of a company. It is calculated by dividing the company's net income by its total number of outstanding shares

Entity – A person, partnership, organization, or business that has a legal and separately identifiable existence

Equity – the value of a property after deduction of charges against it

Escrow – a deed, a bond, money, or a piece of property held in trust by a third party to be turned over to the grantee only upon fulfillment of a condition

Exchange Rate – the value of one currency for the purpose of conversion to another

Exchange-Traded Funds (ETF's) – an investment fund traded on stock exchanges that hold assets such as stocks, commodities, or bonds and generally operates with an arbitrage mechanism designed to keep it trading close to its net asset value

Expense – the cost incurred or required for something

Expense Ratio – a measure of what it costs an investment company to operate an investment fund

Fannie Mae and Freddie Mac – government-sponsored enterprises created by US Congress that buys and guarantees mortgages through the secondary mortgage market. Banks sell to them to free up credit and create more loans

Federal Deposit Insurance Corporation (FDIC) – an independent agency created by Congress to maintain stability and public confidence in the nation's financial system

Federal Housing Administration (FHA) - A government agency that administers many loan programs, loan guarantee programs, and loan insurance programs designed to make housing more available

Federal Reserve – central bank for the US, created on December 23, 1913. The organization is referred to as "the Fed" that operates independently from the US government. It conducts monetary policy, regulates banks, maintains the stability of the financial system, and provides financial services to banks, foreign governments, and the public.

Fiat Currency – currency, such as government notes, not convertible into coin or species of equivalent value

Fiduciary – a person to whom property or power is entrusted for the benefit of another

Finance – to raise or provide funds or capital for

Financial Statement – a summary statement consisting of the income statement, cash flow statement, and balance sheet

Foreign Exchange Market (FOREX or FX) – a global market used to trade currencies

Freedom – the absence of necessity, coercion, or constraint in choice or action

Futures Contracts – financial derivatives that oblige the buyer to purchase some underlying asset or a seller to sell an asset at a predetermined future price and date

Ginnie Mae – a government-owned corporation that guarantees mortgages and mortgage-backed securities from approved lenders

Grant – a sum of money given by an organization for a particular purpose

Gross Income – the total amount an entity earns throughout a certain period

Gross Domestic Product (GDP) – the final value of the goods and services produced within the geographic boundaries of a country during a specified period, normally a year.

Guarantor – Person or firm that endorses a three-party agreement to guarantee the promises made by the first party (the principal) to the second party (client or lender) will be fulfilled, and assumes liability if the principal fails to fulfill them (defaults)

Hedge – An investment made to reduce the risk of adverse price movements in a security

Home Equity Loan – a loan based on the amount of equity a person has in their home

Hyperinflation – extreme economic inflation with prices rising at a very high rate in a very short time

Income - a gain or recurrent benefit usually measured in money that derives from capital or labor

Income Statement – a statement that shows revenues and expenses during a particular period.

Income Tax - **a** tax on any money earned during a fiscal year, usually filed yearly

Individual Retirement Account (IRA) - a tax-advantaged investing tool that individuals use to earmark funds for retirement

Inflation - a general increase in prices and fall in the purchasing value of money

Insurance Premium – the amount of money an individual or business must pay for an insurance policy

Interest Rate - the proportion of a loan that is charged as interest to the borrower, typically expressed as an annual percentage of the loan outstanding

Internal Rate of Return (IRR) – an estimate of a future annual rate of return that should not be confused with actual return on investment

Internal Revenue Service (IRS) - A bureau within the United States Department of the Treasury, the IRS is charged with the responsibility of collecting the taxes imposed by Congress

Intrinsic Value – the true inherent and essential value of an asset independent of its market value

Investment Advisor - a person making investment recommendations in return for a flat fee or percentage of assets managed, known as a commission

Investment Bank – a bank that does not take deposits, but offers financial services and/or advisory-based financial transactions. They can act as intermediaries between security issuers and investors

Joint Venture – a business arrangement where two or more parties pool their resources to accomplish a specific task

Junk Bond –high-yielding, high-risk security, typically issued by a company seeking to raise capital quickly

Keynesian Economics - an economic theory of total spending in the economy and its effects on output and inflation developed by John Maynard Keynes

Lender - an organization or person that lends money or credit

Leverage - the advantageous condition of having a small amount of cost yield a relatively high level of return

Liability Insurance - any insurance policy that protects an individual or business from the risk that they may be sued and held legally liable for something

Line of Credit - an amount of credit extended to a borrower that can be utilized as needed

Liquidity - the ability or ease with which assets can be converted to cash

Loan - a thing that is borrowed, especially a sum of money that is expected to be paid back with interest

Loan to Value (LTV) - the ratio used by lenders to express the ratio of a loan to the value of an asset purchased

Margin - the difference between a product or service's selling price and the cost of production; the ratio of profit to revenue

Money - any object that is generally accepted as payment for goods and services and repayment of debts. The main features of money should be a medium of exchange, a unit of account, and a store of value

Mutual Funds – an open-end professionally managed investment fund that pools money from many investors to purchase securities

Net Income – profit or money received after all expenses have been itemized

Net Operating Income – calculated by subtracting operating expenses from total revenues of a property

Net Present Value (NPV) - the difference between the present value of cash inflows and the present value of cash outflows over a period of time

Net Worth - the value of all financial assets owned by an entity minus the value of all its' outstanding liabilities

Non-Disclosure Agreement (NDA) – a legally binding contract that establishes a confidential relationship

Operating Income – an accounting figure that measures the amount of profit realized from a business's operations, after deducting operating expenses such as wages, depreciation, and cost of goods sold (COGS)

Option – Contract to keep an offer open for a fixed period during which the offeror cannot withdraw the offer

Overdraft – when an individual withdraws more than the current balance from their checking account; a form of finance for businesses that experience fluctuations in working capital

Profit – a financial gain, especially the difference between the amount earned and the amount spent in buying, operating, or producing something

Profit & Loss Statement – a financial statement that summarizes the revenues, costs, and expenses incurred during a specified period, usually a fiscal quarter or year

Pro Forma – Assumed, forecasted, or informal information presented in advance of the actual or formal information. Not to be confused with actual data for an investment

Prospectus – Legally mandated document published by every firm offering its securities to the public for purchase

Real Estate – "real property" that includes the land and anything permanently attached to it, whether natural or man-made

Real Estate Investment Trust (REIT) – Investment vehicle similar to a mutual fund. REITs use the pooled capital of investors to make mortgage loans to builders or developers or to directly invest and manage income-producing property

Return on Equity (ROE) – a measure of the profitability of a business in relation to the equity

Return on Investment (ROI) – a ratio between net profit and the cost of the investment, usually expressed as a percentage. A high ROI means the investments' gains are favorable to its cost

Revenue – The income generated from the sale of goods or services associated with the main operations of an organization before any costs or expenses are deducted

ROTH IRA - A tax-qualified savings account for individuals that allows the account holder to set aside money for retirement. A Roth IRA differs from a traditional IRA in that the contributions to a Roth IRA account are fully taxable at the time they are deposited and that both the principal and the income earned in the account are tax-free when they are withdrawn as distributions

Securities & Exchange Commission (SEC) – US government oversight agency responsible for regulating the securities markets and protecting investors

Stocks – a type of security that represents an ownership share of a company

Stock Exchange – a market in which securities are bought and sold

Surplus – an excess of production or supply

Tax – a compulsory financial charge or some other type of levy imposed on an individual or legal entity by a government organization to fund government spending and various public expenditures

Term Life Insurance – life insurance that provides coverage for a set term and does not accumulate cash surrender value

Trade Deficit – Excess of a nation's imports of goods (tangibles) over its export of goods during a financial year, resulting in a negative balance of trade

Trust Fund – a fund where assets are transferred to be held or managed by single or multiple trustees

Unemployment – a term referring to individuals who are employable and seeking a job but are unable to find a job

Universal Life Insurance - a type of insurance in which the payments of the insured are placed in an investment fund; earnings from which pay the premium on term life insurance while any remainder continues to increase the policy's value

U.S. Dollar Index (USDX) – an index of the value of the United States dollar relative to a basket of foreign currencies

US Treasury – the government department that manages federal finances by collecting taxes, paying bills, and managing currency

Valuation - a quantitative process of determining the fair value of an asset or a firm

Value Added Tax (VAT) – a consumption tax levied on products at every point of sale where value has been added; starting from raw materials to the final retail purchase

Vested - Having full ownership rights, especially after certain conditions such as a period of service have been met

Velocity of Money – Rate at which money circulates, changes hands, or turns over in an economy in a given period

W-2 – a statement prepared annually for employees, showing total gross earnings, Social Security earnings, Medicare earnings, and federal and state taxes withheld from the employee

W-4 – A tax form prepared by an employee for an employer indicating the employee's exemptions and Social Security number, and enabling the employer to determine the amount of taxes to be withheld for the employee

Whole Life Insurance – Life insurance which provides coverage for an individual's whole life, rather than a specified term. A savings component, called cash value or loan value, builds over time and can be used for wealth accumulation

Wire Transfer – a transfer of funds done electronically across a network of banks or transfer agencies around the world

Yield – The annual income earned from an investment, expressed usually as a percentage of the money invested

Zero-Based Budgeting – a method of budgeting in which all expenses must be justified for each new period

FREEDOM SPREADSHEET

The Freedom Spreadsheet is an editable income statement and balance sheet:

https://docs.google.com/spreadsheets/d/e/2PACX-1vSeWOdUQ3YYTIOWQLQiTzv9h5p8JCELOt3S6jNO_sJFbiBub6nZGq8ZSWk3UwkZF5deNKSU_Msv_0S-/pub?output=xlsx

This link should automatically download and open to your device. If not, please visit the Amazon page for this book and look below the description for the most up-to-date link.

RECOMMENDATIONS

While a lot of these resources are finance or mindset related, I believe it is important to find a balance between mind, body, spirit, finance, and relationships. Without balance we will always feel like there is a missing leg on our stool.

I will recommend books that were influential in my life and principles that I believe in or that challenge my beliefs. I have read hundreds of books and listened to many different podcasts / YouTube videos with the below being some that I think are valuable.

Mindset

Think & Grow Rich by Napolean Hill

Man's Search for Meaning by Viktor E. Frankyl

As a Man Thinketh by James Allen

Out of Your Mind by Alan Watts

Atomic Habits by James Clear

7 Habits of Highly Effective People by Steven Covey

Can't Hurt Me by David Goggins

The Seasons of Life by Jim Rohn

Principles by Ray Dalio

How to Win Friends & Influence People by Dale Carnegie

The Road Less Traveled by M. Scott Peck, M.D

The Second Mountain by David Brooks

Stillness is the Key by Ryan Holiday

Ego is the Enemy by Ryan Holiday

Acres of Diamonds by Russell Conwell

The Strangest Secret by Earl Nightingale

The Power of Now by Eckhart Tolle

Subtle Art of Not Giving a F*ck by Mark Manson

Finance & Economics

The Guide to Investing in Gold & Silver by Mike Maloney

Hidden Secrets of Money Series by Mike Maloney on YouTube

Misbehaving: Behavioral Economics by Richard H. Thaler

Currency Wars by James Rickards

Basic Economics by Thomas Sowell

Creature from Jekyll Island by G Edward Griffin

Economics in One Lesson by Henry Hazlitt

The Big Short by Michael Lewis (the movie is also great)

How an Economy Grows & Why it Crashes by Peter Schiff

www.federalreserve.gov

Taxes

The Power of Zero by David McKnight

Tax-Free Wealth by Tom Wheelwright

Top 10 Ways to Avoid Taxes by Josh Shapiro

A Fine Mess by T.R. Reid

The Fair Tax Book by Neal Boortz

Loopholes of Real Estate by Garrett Sutton

www.irs.gov and get a qualified CPA on your team

Wealth Basics / Retirement

Who Moved my Cheese by Dr. Spencer Johnson

The Richest Man in Babylon by George Clason

Cashflow Quadrant by Robert Kiyosaki

The Simple Path to Wealth by JL Collins

The Millionaire Next Door by Thomas Stanley

Passive Income Aggressive Retirement by Rachel Richards

How Much Money Do I Need to Retire by Todd Tresidder

Total Money Makeover by Dave Ramsey

Digital Investing

Investing 101 by Michele Cagan

A Beginners Guide to the Stock Market by Matthew Kratter

How to Day Trade for a Living by Andrew Aziz

How to Make Money in Stock by William O' Neil

The Little Book on Common Sense Investing by John Bogle

The Four Pillars of Investing by William Bernstein

An Altcoin Trader's Handbook by Nik Patel

Cryptoassets: The Investor's Guide by Chris Burniske

www.babypips.com for FOREX Trading

www.sec.gov for laws regarding securities

Life Insurance

Questions and Answers on Life Insurance by Tony Steuer

Money. Wealth. Life Insurance by Jake Thompson

Becoming your Own Banker by R. Nelson Nash

Business Startup & Management

The E Myth Revisited by Michael Gerber

4-Hour Workweek by Timothy Ferris

Start Your Own Business by Entrepreneur Inc.

Start Your Own Corporation by Garrett Sutton

Traction by Gino Wickman

The ONE Thing by Gary Keller

How I Built This by Guy Raz

Rich Dad Poor Dad by Robert Kiyosaki

Entrepreneur Roller Coaster by Darren Hardy

Successful Self-Publishing by Joanna Penn

Built to Sell by John Warrillow

Your Next Five Moves by Patrick Bet-David

Real Estate

Hold by Chader, Doty & Mckissack

Flip by Villani Davis

What Every Real Estate Investor Needs to Know about Cashflow by Gallinelli

Financial Freedom from Real Estate Investing by Michael Blank

Raising Private Capital by Matt Faircloth

The Book on Rental Property Investing by Brandon Turner

Building a Rental Property Empire by Mark Ferguson

Real Estate Investing Gone Bad by Phil Pustejovsky

The Book on Estimating Rehab Costs by J Scott

ABC's of Property Management by Ken McElroy

Millionaire Real Estate Investor by Gary Keller

Podcasts and Media

The Peak Prosperity Podcast with Mike Maloney

Hidden Secrets of Money on YouTube by Mike Maloney

The School of Greatness with Lewis Howes

David Goggins Interviews

REAL AF with Andy Frisella

The Tim Ferris Show

The Joe Rogan Experience

The Cardone Zone by Grant Cardone

Apartment Building Investing with Michael Blank

Bigger Pockets Money Podcast

Bigger Pockets Real Estate Podcast (www.Biggerpockets.com)

The Real Estate Guys Radio Show

Real Estate Strategies Podcast by Ken McElroy

Rich Dad Radio Show by Robert Kiyosaki

The ONE Thing with Geoff Woods

The Science of Success by Matt Bodnar

Optimal Health Daily with Dr. Neal Malik

www.ingramcontent.com/pod-product-compliance
Lightning Source LLC
Chambersburg PA
CBHW070929210326
41520CB00021B/6860